52 Ideas
for Junior Classroom
Assemblies

CHRIS CHESTERTON
AND
PAT GUTTERIDGE

MONARCH
Crowborough

British Library Cataloguing in Publication Data
A catalogue record for this book is available
from the British Library.

ISBN: 1 85424 291 1

Produced by Bookprint Creative Services
P.O.Box 827, BN21 3YJ, England for
MONARCH PUBLICATIONS
Broadway House, The Broadway
Crowborough, East Sussex, TN6 1HQ.
Printed in Great Britain

CONTENTS

*Assemblies marked ** need no preparation or resources*

PART ONE: LEARNING ABOUT LIFE FROM STORIES IN THE OLD TESTAMENT

PART TWO: LEARNING ABOUT LIFE FROM STORIES ABOUT JESUS

PART THREE: LIFE'S BIG QUESTIONS

MATERIAL FOR PHOTOCOPYING FOR PUPILS

INTRODUCTION

HOW TO USE THIS BOOK

The classroom assembly may lack the larger corporate feel and possible musical content of the whole-school assembly, but it also opens up a number of stimulating possibilities. The particular features of the material in *52 Ideas for Junior Classroom Assemblies* include:

➢ minimum preparation for the teacher
➢ visual aids and resources needed are easily available in the classroom
➢ all information needed is supplied in the book
➢ maximum pupil participation
➢ several assemblies include a section for a group to prepare in advance on their own
➢ short, simple plays which pupils will enjoy performing
➢ plenty of open-ended questions to stimulate thought and discussion
➢ themes directly related to children's experience
➢ significant PSE content
➢ stories from the Bible which are integral to the cultural heritage of large parts of the world
➢ complementary up-to-date stories from real life
➢ content fulfilling the 1988 ERA requirement that the majority of acts of worship be 'broadly Christian'.

Many of these assemblies stand on their own, but a number of them tell a story over two or three sessions. This is especially true of Part One, which contains stories from the Old Testament of the Bible. Both Part One and Part Two follow a mainly chronological pattern, but the teacher is free to use them in any order, or to choose a theme relevant to the moment. A number of PSE themes are headlined in the titles, making this easy to do.

It will generally be helpful to check the material a day or so in advance to see whether photocopies or other resources are needed and if pupils are to be involved. A **Background** section gives some historical or cultural facts where this might be helpful to the teacher. The **Life Application** section highlights the relevance of the particular story or series to children's lives.

Often there is a section for a group to prepare. A group which has finished its other work can be chosen. Pupils will enjoy the simple plays, surveys, and craft work in these sections. Most such assemblies need only some photocopies of the relevant section, plus a few normal classroom resources. Occasionally the class as a whole may be asked if anyone can bring a family photo, for example, or some foreign coins from home.

A Clock icon signals the start of the assembly in the text. There may be a story for the teacher to read, or an introduction to the activity, prepared by a group. Most assemblies end with a **Talk/Think about** section. These are designed to stimulate reflection, curiosity, and class discussion. The choice of questions to use will depend on the maturity of the class. The teacher will want to choose not only which questions to use, but also whether to open a question for class discussion or to present it simply for private reflection. It may be that some questions will be returned to later in the day or the week.

The assemblies in Part Three are grouped under the title *Life's Big Questions*. The Westhill Project, as an example, includes *Ultimate Questions* as a key component. These assemblies in particular seek to help pupils explore some of the major questions of life and religion. See the introduction to Part Three for more details.

The 1988 Education Reform Act requires that the majority of school acts of worship be 'broadly Christian'. The aim of this book is to provide the busy teacher with high-quality material to meet that requirement, while giving space for the expression of each individual's own beliefs, doubts and questions. If children are stimulated to think and to move forward in the development of their personal philosophy of life, it will have served its purpose.

PLAN OF A TYPICAL ASSEMBLY OUTLINE

BACKGROUND

Brief notes for the teacher on the context or historical background of the story.

LIFE APPLICATION

How this story or theme relates to a child's world and experience, and what the child might gain from reflecting on it.

RESOURCES

Any items needed for the assembly, such as photocopies of a section for a group to prepare, materials for them to use, and visual aids.

GETTING READY

Notes on any preparations to be made by a group of pupils. This may involve a survey chart to complete, a simple craft project to make a visual aid, or a short play. The photocopiable resources for this are grouped together at the back of the book.

STORY OR INTRODUCTION

A CLOCK icon indicates that the teacher introduces the assembly here. It may start with a simple game, an illustration, or a story. Further sub-headings break the text into sections.

Where a reader or group presentation is introduced this is flashed by a PUPILS icon.

TALK/THINK ABOUT

Questions for class discussion or quiet reflection. This is flashed by a QUESTION MARK icon.

Sometimes a prayer or verse of a poem is included as a further optional stimulus for reflection.

KEY TO ICONS

PUPILS

A point in the assembly where pupils take part.

CLOCK

Start the assembly here.

MASKS

A play for pupils to present.

QUESTION MARK

Questions to talk or think about.

COMPUTER

A verse or prayer that might be printed for display.

CRAFT

A simple craft project for pupils to make a visual aid.

Who is this Jesus?
THE MUSICAL

'A profound experience. What an RE lesson, and a curriculum and PSE triumph!' – Chairman of Governors.

Some of the material in the LEARNING ABOUT LIFE FROM STORIES ABOUT JESUS section was piloted as part of the preparation for a new educational musical for Primary schools, *Who is this Jesus?*

In the musical, two children pose the question, Who is this Jesus? The Book, The Lost Sheep, The Fat Sparrow, The Discarded Crutch and others bring answers from their own experience in the pages of the New Testament. Eight

wonderful songs bring the stories of Jesus to life and give scope for creative expresssion in dance and mime.

These songs are available on tape and can be used in conjunction with some of the assemblies in this book. A production pack containing script, score and CD is available on approval from CENS at the address below. The CD has all the songs, plus backing tracks for use in rehearsal or performance. It also features computer text and graphics files for creating posters, songsheets, etc.

Who is this Jesus? was first performed at The Royal Concert Hall, Nottingham, with eight schools taking part. One Headteacher wrote, 'We have been privileged to be part of something so special and I hope that *Who is this Jesus?* goes on to be performed many more times.'

The cassette and production pack are available from: CENS, 232 Westdale Lane, Carlton, Nottingham NG4 4FW. The cassette costs £4.50, including p. & p. Cheques payable to: CENS. The production pack is sent on approval.

Assembly Line

Fresh and topical ideas for school worship can be found every term in *Assembly Line*. This broadsheet is mailed directly to subscribers at the beginning of term and contains seasonal talks as well as news-related mate-rial. Many people find the mixture of humour, true-life stories, visual appeal and Christian content very helpful.

Assembly Line is edited by 52 IDEAS author Chris Chesterton and is excellent value. For a free sample copy send a large (C5) s.a.e. to Assembly Line, 232 Westdale Lane, Carlton, Nottingham NG4 4FW.

'Assembly Line *arrived this morning – what a tonic! Some really super ideas for new assemblies. Thank you.'* – Primary Headteacher.

PART ONE

LEARNING ABOUT LIFE FROM STORIES IN THE OLD TESTAMENT

LEARNING TO WAIT

THE STORY OF JACOB

OUTLINE PLAN FOR THREE ASSEMBLIES

---

1. THE 'CAN'T WAIT' TWINS

➤ Play for two pupils to prepare
➤ The Jacobs biscuit challenge: eat now or swap for a larger one next time
➤ The story of Jacob and Esau — the 'can't wait' twins
➤ Talk/think about: were the brothers right?

2. JACOB LEARNS PATIENCE

➤ The Jacobs biscuit challenge: part 2
➤ Story: how Jacob had to learn to wait
➤ Talk/think about: am I good at saving things or do I want it all now?

3. WAITING FOR VALUABLE CROPS

➤ Looking at seeds and how long it takes them to grow
➤ How valuable crops in tropical rainforests might be lost through impatience and greed
➤ Talk/think about: what we can do to help
➤ A prayer.

BACKGROUND

Jacob was the son of Isaac and grandson of Abraham, patriarch of both the Jewish and Islamic faiths. He lived c. 1700–1600 BCE. Jacob's story spans a large section of the book of Genesis, beginning in chapter 25. His story exemplifies a familiar biblical theme: 'You reap what you sow', or 'You will be treated in the same way you treat others'. He uses trickery to get what he wants, but is then tricked himself. He is impatient, but is then forced to learn patience.

Behind all this is the theme of God's purpose and promises. God's promise to Abraham was that he would be father to a great nation. This promise begins to see fulfilment as Jacob's name is changed to Israel and as his twelve sons become the founders of the twelve tribes of Israel. Early in the story, Jacob tries to force the pace of history, but his attempts end in failure. God has his own timing.

LIFE APPLICATION

We live in a culture of instant gratification. Sadly, our children may have to learn patience in the DSS queue in years to come, but their present world of TV advertising, especially before Christmas, encourages them to demand what they want and to expect it now. Separation from the agricultural world deprives most of us of the natural rhythm of sowing, waiting, and reaping. We cannot overturn this conditioning in a couple of brief assemblies, but we can hope to prompt a little reflection on the value of learning to wait for good things.

LEARNING TO WAIT 1

TWO IMPATIENT BROTHERS

RESOURCES

- a Jacobs individual biscuit and a larger packet *or* a fun-size and a large Mars or similar
- two copies of the play for two children to prepare in advance
- perhaps a saucepan and spoon from the kitchen.

➤ The Bible story can be found in Genesis 25:19–34.

GETTING READY

Two pupils are needed to act the parts of twin brothers, Jacob and Esau in a play, *The big soup deal.* Photocopiable material is on page 187.

INTRODUCTION: A DIFFICULT CHOICE

Show the class a Jacobs chocolate biscuit (or fun-sized Mars bar or similar). Offer it as an extra snack (to be kept till lunchtime) to a hungry volunteer. Choose one of the eager volunteers to come out to the front and then offer her a choice. She can *either* eat it for lunch today, *or* keep it and wait until the next class assembly and then swap it for a large one. Which will she choose? Show the larger alternative, which you are keeping until the next class assembly.

Ask the rest of the class for a show of hands: which would they do? Could they resist the temptation until next week? After all, a bird in the hand . . .

The question is, are you a 'can't wait' person or a 'wait for something better' person?

STORY: THE 'CAN'T WAIT' TWINS

There is a story in the Bible about two 'can't wait' brothers. They were twins, and their names were Jacob and Esau. Jacob was the younger of the twins; his brother Esau was the first one to be born. Even though he had only been born a few minutes earlier than Jacob, it still meant that Esau would be the head of the family when their father died and that he would get a double share of their father's riches.

But before they were born, God had said something to the twins' mother, Rebekah. He told her that the twins would become the leaders of two nations. The younger twin would be the leader of the stronger nation. As the twins grew up, Jacob was his mum's favourite. She must have often told him what God had said about him and his brother.

So Jacob knew that God had promised to make him the leader of a strong nation. Surely, all he had to do was to wait and see how God's promise would come true. But Jacob was impatient. He was a 'can't wait' person. He wanted to make it happen himself. One day, he got his opportunity. He was making some vegetable soup when his brother Esau came in from hunting in the fields. Esau was a 'can't wait' person, too. Listen to what happened.

PLAY: THE BIG SOUP DEAL

Two children read and act *The big soup deal* which they have prepared.

JACOB	(*He is stirring the soup, tasting it, adding some salt.*)
ESAU	(*Comes in noisily, moaning.*) I didn't catch a thing. Not even a rabbit. And I'm starving. Mmm. That smells good. Hey, Jacob, give me a bowl!
JACOB	Make your own. There's not enough here for you.
ESAU	Oh go on. If I'd caught a rabbit or a partridge, I'd have shared it with you. I've been out since sunrise. I'm weak with hunger.
JACOB	Okay, I'll make a deal with you. I'll sell you some soup.
ESAU	Anything. Just give me some soup.
JACOB	You're the oldest. You'll be head of the family when Dad dies. Sell me the right of the oldest son so that I'll be head of the family.
ESAU	Look, I'm almost dead from hunger. Being the head of the family and all Dad's money won't help me if I die.
JACOB	Right, promise me then.
ESAU	I promise.
JACOB	You promise I can be head of the family and have your share of Dad's money?
ESAU	(*Shouting.*) Yes, I promise. Just give me some soup!

TALK/THINK ABOUT

Do you think either of the brothers was right in what they did?

CONCLUSION

Next time we shall hear what happened to Jacob and about the lesson God gave him in patience.

LEARNING TO WAIT 2
JACOB LEARNS PATIENCE

RESOURCES

• the large Jacobs biscuits or large Mars bar (see previous assembly).

No other preparation is necessary, unless the teacher wants to give Jacob's story to a good reader to read to the class.

➤ The Bible story can be found in Genesis, chapters 29 to 32.

INTRODUCTION: COULD SHE WAIT?

Show the large biscuits or Mars bar. Has the person who was given the small one last time kept it to swap? Could she wait? If so, swap for the larger one and ask her how she felt about waiting. Was she tempted to eat it? If she has eaten it, ask her to say how she feels now.

Last time we heard the story of the 'can't wait' twins. Jacob persuaded his twin brother Esau to sell him the right to be head of the family and his share of their father's riches. But actually, Jacob never got either! Listen to his own story of what happened. (This might be read by a really good reader.)

JACOB'S STORY

When my father was very old, I tricked him into believing that I was Esau. Father gave me the blessing as the new head of the family. Esau was so angry when he found out that he wanted to kill me! The only thing I could do was to run away. Mum told me to go and stay with uncle Laban, hundreds of miles away in another country.

So I went to live with my uncle. I earned my keep by looking after his sheep. Uncle Laban had two daughters, Leah and Rachel. Rachel was the younger sister, and she was very beautiful. I soon fell in love with her. I went to Laban and said, 'Let me marry Rachel. If you do, I will work for you for seven years.'

Laban agreed. I worked hard for seven years looking after the sheep, but it did not seem too long because I was so much in love with Rachel. I was beginning to learn that it is worth waiting for something good.

At last came the wedding day. There were lots of guests and a great feast. The bride came in her beautiful eastern dress with all her fine jewellery. As was the custom, she wore a veil over her face. When the wedding ceremony was ended and we were married, my bride lifted her veil. What a shock! It was Leah, not Rachel! Uncle Laban had tricked me into marrying the wrong sister. I was furious. 'What have you done to me?' I shouted. 'I worked hard for you so that I could marry Rachel! Why did you trick me?'

'In our country,' replied Uncle Laban, 'we don't let the younger sister marry before the older sister. Now, I am willing to let you marry Rachel as well, and have them both as your wives. But you must work for me another seven years.'

Seven more years! What could I do? I had to agree. Years before, I tricked Dad. Now my uncle had tricked me. I suppose it served me right! Now I'd got to wait seven more years to be the head of my own family. Seven years and seven years — how many years did I have to wait altogether?

THE END OF THE STORY

Does anyone remember the promise God made to Rebekah before the twins were born? They would both become leaders of nations, and Jacob's nation would be stronger than Esau's. In the end, it came true. Esau's family became a nation called Edom. Edom existed for some centuries, but it has long since disappeared from the map of the world.

And Jacob? He had twelve sons and several daughters. After many years he finally went back to his old home and made peace with his brother Esau. One day in a vision, God gave him a new name. Instead of Jacob, his name was to be Israel. Have you heard that name before? After that time, the people in the Bible were called, 'the children of Israel.' The nation of Israel is still often in the news on TV today. Israel: named after a 'can't wait' person who learned the hard way how to be a 'wait for something better' person.

TALK/THINK ABOUT

1. When you have a lot of sweets and chocolate for Christmas or a birthday, do you eat them all at once or make them last?

2. Do you spend all your pocket-money, or save some of it to buy something special?

LEARNING TO WAIT 3

WAITING FOR VALUABLE CROPS

INTRODUCTION: THE FARMER WAITS PATIENTLY

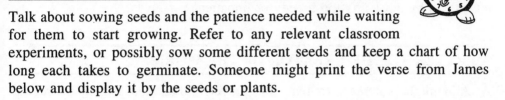

Talk about sowing seeds and the patience needed while waiting for them to start growing. Refer to any relevant classroom experiments, or possibly sow some different seeds and keep a chart of how long each takes to germinate. Someone might print the verse from James below and display it by the seeds or plants.

A man called James, who was probably a brother of Jesus, wrote this in a letter in the Bible: **'See how the farmer waits for the land to yield its valuable crop and how patient he is.'** (James 5:7)

VALUABLE RAINFOREST CROPS

Valuable crops do not just grow from the seeds people plant. They might already be growing in rainforests, but no-one has discovered them yet. There might be plants we don't know about that can cure diseases. In 1994, for example, a soldier who got lost in a rainforest had a dangerous infection cured by a local person using a mixture made from some plants that grow there.

We all know about what is happening to some of the tropical rainforests. Areas of trees are being cut down and burned to grow grass for cattle. After a couple of years, the soil is exhausted. The grass is too poor to feed the cattle, so the farmer moves on to a new area and cuts down more trees. In other places there are vast mines and quarries. The forest is turned into near-desert. Not only do lots of animals die, but plants that might provide new medicines to heal diseases are being wiped out.

The world is full of 'can't wait' people like this. Sometimes it is not their fault. A poor farmer may be forced to live like this because no-one is offering him and his family any other choice. But often it is just greed. Greedy people want to make money now and don't care what sort of mess they leave behind them.

TALK/THINK ABOUT

1. Some people really can't wait. If they don't get food or money to feed their families, they will die. What can we do to help them?

2. Some people would say that God has given us a world full of valuable crops of all different kinds. Do you agree? Are there ways in which we can help look after them by not being too greedy or impatient ourselves?

A PRAYER TO THE CREATOR OF THE WORLD

A child might volunteer to read this prayer. Others can join in by saying 'Amen', if they wish.

Great Creator God,
You took millions of years to prepare this earth for us.
Help us to care for it by learning to be patient and only taking what we need.
Amen.

STRENGTH AND WEAKNESS

THE STORY OF GIDEON

OUTLINE PLAN FOR TWO ASSEMBLIES

1. A NERVOUS LEADER

➤ Two pupils prepare a TV interview in which Gideon explains a scientific experiment asking God for answers

➤ Questions about the story

➤ Talk/think about feeling scared.

2. GIDEON LEARNS TO SUBTRACT AND DIVIDE

➤ Group prepares pot and torch visual aids in advance

➤ Story for the teacher to tell with mathematical illustrations and help from the group

➤ Talk/think about good ideas to stop bullying and fighting.

BACKGROUND

The story of Gideon is found in the book of Judges, chapters 6 to 8. Gideon was the youngest son of Joash, a member of a not-very-powerful tribe. He was totally lacking in military training or experience of leadership. In around 1100 BCE a warlike Bedouin tribe, the Midianites, invaded Israel from the east. Riding on camels gave them a decisive military advantage. Lacking a strong leader, many of the Israelites had fled to the mountains. The Bible record depicts God choosing Gideon to rally his people and to lead a tiny group of them to a memorable victory over their oppressors.

LIFE APPLICATION

These assemblies aim to show that strength is not always the most important factor. Bullies and gangs do not have to have the upper hand. The story of Gideon shows that weak people with good ideas — in this case God's ideas — can overcome those with the greater physical strength. This provides an opportunity to review means used in the school to combat bullying and fighting.

STRENGTH AND WEAKNESS 1

A NERVOUS LEADER

RESOURCES

- two copies of the TV interview for two pupils to prepare in advance
- a table, two chairs, a microphone (eg ball of wool on the end of a stick), a woolly jumper.

GETTING READY

Two pupils are needed to act out a TV interview between an interviewer and Gideon. Photocopiable material is on pages 188 to 190.

INTRODUCTION: GIDEON'S TV INTERVIEW

Today we are going to watch a TV interview which two members of the class have prepared. It's about a story in the Bible that happened more than 3,000 years ago. Of course, TV wasn't invented then, but it's a different way of looking at the story, and helps us to understand the main character.

His name was Gideon and he lived at a frightening time. His country had been invaded by a warlike tribe called the Midianites and a lot of the people had run away to the mountains. Gideon himself was too frightened to carry on his normal life. At the start of the story he was hiding in a stone trough used to crush grapes to make wine. An angel came to him and told Gideon that God wanted him to be the new leader for Israel. Gideon could hardly believe it, but he sent out a call to the people to join him. Then he set up an experiment, just to make sure that it really was God talking to him and not his imagination. Now let's listen to the interview.

PLAY: GIDEON'S EXPERIMENT

The TV interview prepared by pupils.

INTERVIEWER   Welcome to Newsworld. The latest news from the war zone is that the Midianites are continuing their invasion and stealing all the food they can find. Many people have run away, too frightened to fight.

But there are some promising signs. As we reported yesterday, a young man called Gideon has issued a call to people to join him in resisting the invaders. He also seems to be something of a scientist. We have invited him into the studio this evening. Mr. Gideon, welcome to Newsworld.

GIDEON   (*Comes in and sits down very nervously*) Er, thank you. Good, um, evening.

INTERVIEWER   Well, Mr. Gideon, I understand this all started in a winepress. That sounds rather strange. Were you making wine?

GIDEON   Er, no.

INTERVIEWER   Well, some new jam using grapes perhaps?

GIDEON   Er, not exactly.

INTERVIEWER   Well, what were you doing in that winepress?

GIDEON   Threshing wheat, sir.

INTERVIEWER   Wheat? To make flour? In a winepress?

GIDEON   Er, yes, yes . . .

INTERVIEWER   Is this some new scientific invention?

GIDEON   Er, no, not really. You see, I was scared.

INTERVIEWER   So you were hiding in a winepress?

GIDEON   Yes, so they wouldn't get me. Those Midianites. They're such bullies. No one can stand up to them.

INTERVIEWER   Yes, quite, I understand. You were hiding in the winepress so your wheat would not get stolen. Let's move on quickly to the experiment with the woolly jumper. Do you have it with you? (*Gideon shows the woolly jumper.*)

Thank you. Perhaps you can explain to the viewers what you did with this jumper.

GIDEON   (*More confidently.*) Well it all started when God told me . . .

INTERVIEWER   (*Interrupting.*) Excuse me, you said **God** — was he in this experiment?

GIDEON   Oh very much so, sir (*growing in confidence*). God told me to lead the Israelites against the Midianites.

INTERVIEWER   But I thought you were, um, scared of the enemy?

GIDEON   I am. I mean, I was. Well, that was before . . . now I know that God is with me.

INTERVIEWER   How do you know?

GIDEON   Well, I thought God was telling me to lead the Israelites, and I was frightened. But the idea wouldn't go away, so I decided on an experiment. (*Picks up jumper and demonstrates.*)

You see, I said to God, 'I'll leave this on the ground overnight. In the morning, if the ground is dry and the woolly jumper is wet with dew, then I will know that I must lead Israel.'

INTERVIEWER   And was the jumper wet?

GIDEON   Yes.

INTERVIEWER   And the ground was dry?

GIDEON   Yes.

INTERVIEWER   So, what did you decide then?

GIDEON   To do it again.

INTERVIEWER   That sounds like good scientific practice!

GIDEON   Yes, but I changed it a bit. I said to God, 'This time, make the jumper dry and the ground wet.'

INTERVIEWER   And what happened this second time?

GIDEON   The jumper was dry and the ground was wet.

INTERVIEWER   Very interesting, Mr. Gideon. As a result of those experiments what are you going to do?

GIDEON   I'm going to lead the Israelites against the Midianites, with God's help. In fact, I want everyone who is listening and prepared to stand up against these bullies to meet me tomorrow.

INTERVIEWER   Thank you. (*Turning to face the audience.*) So could this be a turning point in the struggle against the Midianites? Can young Gideon really free us from this menace? We'll keep you informed of all the latest news here on Newsworld. Good night.

QUESTIONS

Some questions to ask the class to check on their understanding of the story.

1. Where had Gideon been hiding and why?

2. How was he feeling then?

3. What experiment did Gideon tell the interviewer about?

4. Who did Gideon say was helping him?

5. How had Gideon changed by the end of the interview?

TALK/THINK ABOUT

1. Do you feel scared sometimes? What kind of things scare you?

2. Do you hide when you feel scared?

3. Some people believe that God can help them. Next time we shall find out about how God helped Gideon against the Midianites. Does anyone have any other stories about how God helped someone who was scared?

STRENGTH AND WEAKNESS 2
GIDEON LEARNS TO SUBTRACT AND DIVIDE

RESOURCES

- photocopies of pot and torch visual aids for a group to make one each in advance. Photocopiable illustrations are on page 191
- scissors, crayons or felt-tips, glue
- a blackboard and chalk for the mathematics.

GETTING READY

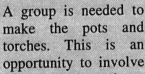

A group is needed to make the pots and torches. This is an opportunity to involve a group with weaker reading skills. They will need to paste the drawings of the pots and torches onto card, cut them out and colour them. Photocopiable material is on page 191.

They will be needed during the assembly to help act out the end part of the story of Gideon and the Midianites. They must each have their torch hidden behind their pot. At the right time, you will ask them to stand round the class, make a noise like a trumpet, show the torches and hold them up, and then shout, 'For the Lord and for Gideon!'

STORY: HOW GIDEON BEAT THE MIDIANITES

We found out last time that God chose Gideon to lead the frightened Israelites against the Midianite bullies. He had called the people together, and they set off to meet the enemy. But God didn't want the Israelites to think they had won by their own strength. They might start boasting and forget him. God wanted them to be absolutely sure that he had won the battle for them.

So he started teaching Gideon some mathematics!

THE FIRST STEP

There were 32,000 men in the Israelite army. God said, 'Anyone who is frightened can go home.' So 22,000 went home. How many did that leave? (Do the sum on the board.) 10,000.

THE SECOND STEP

God said, 'There are still too many. I'll set them a test. Send them to the river for a drink. Watch them! I only want those who are watchful, who bend and cup their hands to pick up the water. Those who get down on their knees can go home.'

Gideon watched. There were 9,700 men who got down on their knees and put their mouths to the water to drink. Gideon sent them home. How many were left? (Do the sum on the board.) Only 300. But listen: before the 9,700 went home, Gideon collected enough spare water pots and ram's horn trumpets for each of his 300 men to have one.

THE THIRD STEP

According to the story there were 135,000 Midianites and now only 300 Israelites! That is one Israelite for every 450 Midianites. Write on board: 300 to 135,000 or one Israelite to 450 Midianites. Pretty frightening!

Gideon gave each one of these 300 Israelite men a trumpet, a water pot, and some wood and rags to make a burning torch. We don't have 300 children in the class, but one group has made some pots. We'll ask them to stand up at the front of the class. They have to be ready to make trumpet noises when I tell them, and show their pots. We will pretend that the rest of the class are the Midianites, the enemy.

THE FOURTH STEP

So Gideon was left with only 300 men. Then God wanted them divided into three groups. How many in each group? (Do the sum on the board.) A hundred.

Gideon took one group to one side of the enemy camp in the middle of the night. That is these people at the front. The other groups took up their positions around the camp. When Gideon gave the signal, they all blew their trumpets and smashed their pots. Inside the pots were burning torches. They all shouted, 'For the Lord and for Gideon!' (Get the group to act this out.)

The Midianites were terrified. They woke up in the dark to find fire, men shouting, and trumpets blaring all around them. They thought they were surrounded by a great army. In the confusion they started to fight each other and to run away.

The Israelites had won — with God's help! The Midianites never caused them any more trouble, and the land of Israel had peace for forty years, as long as Gideon was alive.

TALK/THINK ABOUT

That was fun, but more than that, it showed that strength is not always the answer. A small weak army with good ideas beat a large strong army. Good ideas can be better problem solvers than violence.

What good ideas have we got in our school to stop bullying and fighting?

HELPING SOMEONE IN NEED
THE STORY OF RUTH

BACKGROUND

The story of Ruth takes place during the time of the Judges, between the return from Egypt and Saul becoming the first king of Israel. It concerns ordinary people, but an extraordinary tale of devotion. Although Ruth is a native of Moab, east of the Dead Sea, she is prepared to leave the security of her own family and go to an uncertain future in Israel with her mother-in-law after the death of her husband. Her subsequent marriage to Boaz in Bethlehem leads to her becoming an ancestor of two more famous sons of Bethlehem, David and Jesus.

RESOURCES

♦ copies of the letters for three readers to prepare.

GETTING READY

Three pupils are needed to read some imaginary letters to a problem page in a newspaper. There are three letters to read: from Ruth, from the Editor, and from Boaz. Photocopiable material is on pages 192 to 193.

INTRODUCTION: *THE ISRAELI TIMES* PROBLEM PAGE

Newspapers and magazines did not exist in Bible times, but let's imagine that they did. Imagine there was an *Israeli Times* with a page near the back for readers' problems. Listen to what one reader wrote to the problem page and the reply she got.

Three pupils read the problem-page letters and reply.

35

FIRST LETTER

Dear Sir,

I am a young woman from Moab, living with my mother-in-law in Israel. Her name is Naomi. My husband has died, but I won't go back to my own country as my mother-in-law would have no-one to look after her. Now we are very poor and worried because we have nothing to eat. What shall we do?

Yours sincerely,

Ruth.

ANSWER IN THE NEWSPAPER

Dear Ruth,

I am sorry to hear of the difficulties you are having since your husband died. But it is good to read your letter and discover your kindness to your mother-in-law, Naomi. Not many young women are as faithful as you are these days. I am sure God will bless you because of your kindness and show you the way forward. Listen to your mother-in-law's advice, because she is older and wiser than you, and God will speak through her. Please let us know how you get on.

Yours sincerely,

The Editor.

THIRD LETTER

Dear Sir,

Some time ago, a young woman called Ruth wrote to you with a problem. I want you to know that your advice to her was very good. All her problems are solved, because she is now my dear and beautiful wife! Let me explain what happened.

Naomi is my cousin. She returned to our village of Bethlehem after living in another country for several years. It was a sad time, because her husband had died and then her son, Ruth's first husband, also died. She felt very bitter. If it had not been for Ruth, I don't know what she would have done.

I first saw Ruth when she was collecting fallen grains of barley in my field. It was all she and Naomi had to live on. I told my workers to leave some corn for her so they would have enough to eat. As the days of the harvest passed, I grew to admire Ruth and then to love her. Finally, I asked her to marry me.

It was only later that I learned that my cousin Naomi had been scheming to bring us together. It was Naomi who advised Ruth to collect the barley in my field and make sure that I noticed her. I am very glad she did! You were quite right to tell Ruth to listen to her mother-in-law's advice.

Yours gratefully,

Boaz.

CONCLUSION

The story of Ruth is famous because Ruth put someone else first, and not herself. It would have been easy for her to go back to her own family when her husband died. That was the usual thing to do. But Ruth was prepared to go to a strange country to look after her mother-in-law. Through this act of kindness she got herself a very good husband, Boaz. Later, she became the great-grandmother of David, who killed Goliath.

Here is the famous promise that Ruth made to Naomi.

Every place you go, I will go. Every place you live, I will live. Your people will be my people. Your God will be my God. And where you die, I will die. And there I will be buried. I ask the Lord to punish me terribly if I do not keep this promise: only death will separate us. (Ruth 1:16–17)

TALK/THINK ABOUT

1. Ruth went to live in a foreign country and took on the customs of another people. Have you lived in another country? Have you tried other peoples' customs?

2. Ruth stayed with Naomi when she was in trouble. Would you stay with someone in trouble, perhaps someone in the playground today?

HEARING AND DOING
THE STORY OF THE BOY SAMUEL

OUTLINE PLAN FOR FOUR ASSEMBLIES

1. HANNAH'S PRAYER

➤ Story for the teacher or a good reader to read
➤ Questions on the story.

2. THE BOYS WHO WOULD NOT LISTEN

➤ Group to prepare a Time-Traveller's Report and to improvise a play
➤ Life-Application question for reflection.

3. SAMUEL HEARS AND OBEYS

➤ Story for the teacher to read with two pupils playing Samuel and Eli
➤ Questions on the story.

4. ARE YOU LISTENING? Life Application.

➤ A group prepares a 'radio play' tape story about a child who hears the Green Cross Code but does not put it into practice.

BACKGROUND

Samuel was the last of Israel's leaders (traditionally, 'judges') before Saul was chosen as the first king of Israel. He was also a great prophet, the first since Moses. In this series of assemblies we think about his birth in around 1075 BCE and his childhood. The story of the child Samuel in the Temple hearing God call him is a well-loved one. At this time the Temple was in reality the tabernacle or tent which the Israelites had carried with them in their journey from Egypt. It had been set up at Shiloh, 30 km north of Jerusalem, and housed the Ark of the Covenant which contained the Ten Commandments written on two stone tablets. The Temple and the Ark were the visible signs of the presence of God.

We finish our story when the Ark has been captured by Israel's enemies, the

Philistines. Pupils might like to know that such great disasters befell the Philistines while they held the Ark that they returned it to Israel just seven months later. The full story is in 1 Samuel, chapter 5 and 6.

LIFE APPLICATION

The theme of hearing and doing jumps out of the pages of this story. Hannah's husband, Elkanah, hears his wife's sorrow at not having a child, but can only be sympathetic. Eli, the priest, mishears at first and adds to her hurt. God hears Hannah and answers her prayer. Eli's two sons refuse to do what their father tells them and bring disaster on themselves, whilst the boy Samuel hears and obeys. The name Samuel even means, 'God heard'!

The first assembly in this series focuses on hearing; pupils are encouraged to listen carefully to the story so that they can answer questions about it after. The second tells the story of the priest's sons who hear but refuse to obey. Pupils are asked to think of occasions when it is vital not just to hear but to do, eg swimming lessons. The third asks pupils to reflect on the contrast between what happened to the boy who listened and obeyed and to the boys who would not listen. In the fourth a group of pupils imagines the consequences to a child who ignores the Green Cross Code.

HEARING AND DOING 1
HANNAH'S PRAYER

RESOURCES

None needed.

INTRODUCTORY ACTIVITY

Focus on the theme by using one of these activities:

➤ Chinese Whispers. Form a line of half-a-dozen volunteers. Whisper an instruction to the first, who then whispers it to the second, and so on. The last in line must carry out the instruction

➤ Simon Says. Play sitting in places. Each child has five lives and loses one when they make a mistake. (This keeps everyone involved.) Finish as soon as the game has gone on long enough and see how many lives pupils have left. Use instructions like: 'touch . . . '; 'scratch . . . '; 'hold . . . '; 'close . . . '; 'open . . . '; 'nod/shake your head';'stop'. Get the class to co-operate in seeing how quietly you can talk but still keeping the game going (but be aware of pupils with hearing difficulties).

STORY: HANNAH'S PRAYER

Are you a good listener? For our next three class assemblies we have a story where listening and hearing right was very important. The story begins more than 3,000 years ago in Israel. In this part of the story you will hear about a woman who was very sad. Three people heard her: one listened and was kind but could not help, one did not hear right and was rude, and one heard and helped her. See if you can be really good listeners and tell me who these three were when we finish.

Hannah was very sad. She had a kind husband, Elkanah, who loved her very much, but she did not have any children. In those days it was thought to be a great disgrace if a wife could not have a baby. Hannah knew others talked about her behind her back. Sometimes they even said spiteful things to her face.

Every year she and Elkanah went to worship God in the Temple at Shiloh. And every year, at the special meal they ate, Hannah would find she could not hold back her tears. 'Why are you crying?' Elkanah would say to her. 'Please don't be miserable. Don't I mean more to you than ten children?' But nothing could cheer her up.

Once, when they had finished the meal, Hannah got up and went to a quiet corner of the Temple courtyard on her own. The priest was sitting on a chair by the Temple doorway. His name was Eli. He watched as floods of tears poured down Hannah's cheeks. She was praying silently and earnestly to the Lord God for a baby. 'Great and powerful God,' she prayed, 'if you will only see my distress and give me a son, then I will give him back to you to serve you all the days of his life.'

Eli could see Hannah's lips moving, but not hear what she was saying. 'She's drunk!' he thought. 'Fancy coming to the Temple when she has had too much wine!' He gave her a good telling-off. Poor Hannah had to explain that she was very upset, not drunk. Eli was sorry then, and spoke kindly to her.

Elkanah took Hannah home again. Not long after, there was the best possible news: Hannah was going to have a baby. 'Oh, thank you, Lord God,' said Hannah. 'I asked you for this baby and you heard me.' Hannah felt she was the happiest woman in the world.

When the baby was born, Hannah called him Samuel. The name Samuel means, 'God heard.' Hannah did not go to the Temple that year with Elkanah. She was too busy looking after baby Samuel.

QUESTIONS

Who has been a good listener?

1. Why was Hannah sad? (She had no children)

2. Who said kind things and tried to make her feel better? (Elkanah)

3. Who was rude because he did not hear properly? (Eli)

4. Who did Hannah ask to help her? (God)

5. Why did Hannah call her baby Samuel? (It means 'God heard')

HEARING AND DOING 2

THE BOYS WHO WOULD NOT LISTEN

RESOURCES

- copies of the Time-Traveller's script and the play outline for a group to prepare in advance
- materials from the scrap-box to make Time-Travellers headgear
- a large fork, used for spearing meat in a pot, and bowl or box as the pot of meat — to make or borrow from the kitchen.

GETTING READY

At least five pupils are needed. They have three things to do:

1. Make a Time-Traveller's helmet

2. Practice reading a report by a Time-Traveller

3. Four of them make up a short play.

Photocopiable material is on pages 194 to 196.

INTRODUCTION: THE TEMPLE AT SHILOH

Last time we had the story of Hannah and her baby, Samuel. Who remembers the name of the priest at the Temple at Shiloh? . . . Eli. Eli had two sons with funny names, Hophni and Phineas. These two boys certainly heard what was said to them, but they did not want to do it. They were training to be priests like their father, but the way they treated the people who came to the Temple was unfair. We shall find out what they did in a minute.

When this story took place, more than 3,000 years ago, people used to go to the Temple to offer a sacrifice to God. Most of us don't keep our own cows and sheep and chickens at home for food. Some of us may not eat meat at all. The only animals we have are pets. So we find it hard to understand killing animals for food or for a sacrifice. To help us, we need a Time-Traveller to go back 3,000 years and tell us what it was like then.

43

TIME-TRAVELLER'S REPORT

A pupil presents the Time-Traveller's report.

- ☒ The date is 1,000 years before Jesus was born.
- ☒ Place: some hills in Israel. It is hot. The grass is brown.
- ☒ I can see some big, square tents. Some women in the tents are making bread. The bread looks like fat pancakes.
- ☒ I can see some children. They don't go to school. They are in the hills. They are looking after little flocks of sheep and goats. I think they do that all day long.
- ☒ Now I can see a family. They are walking along a dusty track. They are taking a sheep with them. It looks like the fattest sheep in the flock.
- ☒ The family arrives at the Temple at Shiloh. They have come to say thank you to God for looking after them. They also want to say sorry for the wrong things they have done. They give the sheep to the priest for a sacrifice. It's like giving something back to God.
- ☒ The priest has to be a butcher. He cuts up the meat and burns some of the best meat on a fire on the altar. Then he puts the rest in a big pot to boil as a stew.
- ☒ When the meat is cooked, the priest comes with a big fork. He sticks it in the pot and spears a big piece of meat. That is the share for him and his children.
- ☒ The family sits down and eats the rest of the stew. It's like a party. They all feel happy because they have said thank you to God and sorry to God. The sacrifice shows they really mean it.
- ☒ End of report. Returning to the present.

TEACHER'S LINK

The priest at Shiloh, Eli, had those two sons with funny names: Hophni and Phineas. One of their jobs was to stick the big fork in the pot and spear a piece of meat. It was like a lucky dip. But watch this play now and see what they did.

PLAY: LUCKY DIP

Group presents the play: *Lucky dip*.

Scene 1:

A VISITOR (or a family) comes to the Temple to offer a sacrifice. HOPHNI and PHINEAS say they want their portion. The visitor says they can take their lucky-dip from the pot with the big fork as normal. HOPHNI and PHINEAS say they want the best steak or the best joint for roasting, not just any old piece of boiled meat. They threaten to beat the visitor up if they don't get what they want.

Scene 2:

The visitor goes to ELI, the priest. He is upset because he has come to pray to God and offer a sacrifice, but he is being bullied. Hophni and Phineas are breaking God's laws. ELI is shocked and says he will speak to his sons.

Scene 3:

ELI tells HOPHNI and PHINEAS off. They are hurting other people and that makes God unhappy, too. Who will protect them if they break God's laws like this? When ELI leaves, the two boys laugh at the old man behind his back. They are not going to listen to him. They decide to go on demanding the best pieces of meat.

TALK ABOUT

Hophni and Phineas heard what their father told them to do, but they decided not to do it. Can we think of times in school when it might be harmful to hear what is said to us but not do it? Eg swimming lessons: what are we told to do if the hooter sounds? What might happen if we don't do it?

HEARING AND DOING 3
SAMUEL HEARS AND OBEYS

RESOURCES

- copies of the story for two good readers to play the parts of Eli and Samuel while the teacher reads the text.

GETTING READY

Give two pupils copies of this story and have them play the parts of Samuel and Eli. They may need prompting if this is done without rehearsal. To help set the scene, dim the room by drawing curtains or blinds. (But leave enough light to read by!) Photocopiable material is on pages 197 to 198.

THE STORY

We left the story of Hannah and Samuel soon after Samuel was born. What did the name Samuel mean? . . . 'God heard'. Hannah made God a promise if he answered her prayer for a baby. Does anyone remember what the promise was? . . . She promised the child would serve God all the days of his life.

Hannah did not forget her promise. When Samuel was old enough, she took him to the Temple to be Eli's special helper. Old Eli was nearly blind, so there were lots of jobs for Samuel to do. Eli's own two sons, Hophni and Phineas, were far too selfish to help their father.

Samuel grew to love Eli, but he also looked forward to his parents' visits. Each year Hannah brought him some new clothes she had made. And nearly every year there was a new brother or sister for him to meet.

At night, Samuel slept in the Temple. Just a few metres away, behind a thick curtain, was the most holy thing in all Israel. It was a beautiful box covered in pure gold called the Ark. Inside were the two stone tablets with the Ten

Commandments carved on them. Samuel would never have dared peep around that curtain, but he wasn't afraid sleeping alone in the dark Temple. He just knew that he was in the safest place he could possibly be.

PLAY

TEACHER	One night he woke up to hear his name being called. 'Samuel!'
SAMUEL	(*Sitting up*) Here I am. (*Getting up and going to Eli*) Here I am. You called me.
ELI	I didn't call you. Go back and lie down again. (*Samuel lies down again*)
TEACHER	Samuel supposed he must have been dreaming. He was just dropping off to sleep when he heard his name being called again, 'Samuel!'
SAMUEL	(*Getting up and going to Eli*) Here I am. You called me.
ELI	I didn't call you. Go back and lie down again.
TEACHER	Then it happened a third time. By now Eli was wide awake. He realised that it must be God calling the boy. 'Samuel!'
SAMUEL	(*Getting up and going to Eli*) Here I am. You called me.
ELI	Go back and lie down again. And if he calls you again say, 'Speak, Lord, for your servant is listening.' (*Samuel lies down again*)
TEACHER	I wonder how Samuel felt as he went back to lie down on his mat this time? He didn't have long to wait. 'Samuel! Samuel!' said the voice.
SAMUEL	Speak, for your servant is listening.
TEACHER	Then God began to speak to Samuel. It was a hard message.

God was angry because of the way Hophni and Phineas had treated the sacrifices and the people who came to the Temple to worship God. He was angry that Eli had let his sons go on doing it and not stopped them. They had been warned, but they had not listened to the warnings. Now God could not let it go on any longer.

The next day Eli called Samuel and asked him what God had said to him. Samuel was scared to give Eli God's message, but he knew he had to tell the truth. He told Eli everything.

Not long after that there was a battle between the Israelites and their enemies, the Philistines. Because they were losing the battle, the Israelites sent to Shiloh to get the golden Ark. They thought if they had the Ark God would be with them and help them win the battle. Hophni and Phineas came from the Temple with the Ark. But instead of winning the battle, they lost. The Philistines captured the Ark, and both Hophni and Phineas were killed. When Eli heard the news he was so shocked that he fell off his chair and died.

That was a terrible day. Many of the people must have thought God had deserted them. But he hadn't. As Samuel grew up, God continued to speak to him. It says in the Bible that Samuel remembered everything God said to him. The people saw that Samuel was a man who listened to God and they made him their leader. He was one of the wisest leaders they ever had.

QUESTIONS

Who has been a good listener?

1. What was the golden box in the Temple called and what was inside it? (The Ark, and the two stone tablets with the Ten Commandments carved on them)

2. Who was really calling Samuel in the middle of the night? (God)

3. Why do you think Samuel was scared to tell Eli God's message? (It said God was angry with Eli and his sons)

4. Why was the day of the battle a terrible day? (Israel lost the battle and the Ark was captured)

5. Why was Samuel a very good leader of the people of Israel when he grew up? (He listened to God)

HEARING AND DOING 4
ARE YOU LISTENING?

RESOURCES

* a tape-recorder, microphone, and tape
* copies of the radio-play instructions for a group to prepare.

GETTING READY

A group of pupils is needed to make up a play for the next class assembly and record it like a radio play. The play is about the Green Cross Code and someone who did not listen properly. The group may need an adult helper. Photocopiable material is on pages 198 to 199.

INTRODUCTION

Introduce the play by reminding the children of what happened in the last part of the story of Samuel and Eli's family. One group has prepared an up-to-date play about someone who heard something important but did not do it.

PLAY

The group presents their radio play.
Scene 1:

You could start with one person being the Police School Liaison Officer coming into school to remind pupils about the Green Cross Code. Someone else could be the teacher reminding everybody to remember what they heard when they go home.

Scene 2:

It is home time, with people shouting goodbye to each other. There could be an ice-cream van outside school – can somebody play ice-cream van music on a xylophone or recorder?

49

Scene 3:

Two children could be talking about buying an ice-cream. One says to remember the Green Cross Code but the other is in too much of a hurry. There is an accident. Can you make noises like a car skidding and an ambulance coming?

Scene 4:

You could have a scene at the hospital, or a reporter asking people what happened, or the head teacher talking in assembly the next day.

Could you make up a jingle to finish with to remind people to use the Green Cross Code?

SUMMING UP THE SERIES ON LISTENING

A wise saying of King Solomon:

Pay attention and listen to what wise people say. Remember what I am teaching you. (Proverbs 22:17)

A pupil might print this on the computer and display it on the wall.

LIVING IN FAMILIES
THE STORY OF DAVID

OUTLINE PLAN FOR FOUR ASSEMBLIES

1. DEALING WITH BULLIES

➤ The story of David, his older brother, and Goliath
➤ Talk/think about being picked on and how to respond.

2. A GOOD FRIEND

➤ The story of David and Jonathan
➤ Talk/think about friends, brothers and sisters.

3. HELP FROM THE FAMILY

➤ The story of David and his wives
➤ Talk/think about helping each other in families.

4. DAVID'S TERRIBLE CRIME

➤ The story of David and Uriah
➤ A true story of a boy who shot a horse
➤ Talk/think about what to do if something dreadful happens.

BACKGROUND

David — slayer of Goliath, writer of 'The Lord is my Shepherd', founder of Jerusalem as the spiritual capital of Israel, father of the family from which would come the Messiah — every child should know this man and his story. It is very much a 'warts and all' story and shows how God can use people despite their failings.

After his defeat of the Philistine champion Goliath, David was at first welcomed at court by King Saul and married Saul's daughter, Michal. But the king's fits of jealous rage forced David into hiding, and he became the leader of a group of outlaws. When Saul was killed in a battle with the

51

Philistines around 1010 BCE, David was made king and reigned for forty years, uniting the Hebrew people and consolidating their hold on the land.

David's life is rich in stories. The four presented here focus on David as a member of a family. King David is imagined in his old age looking back as if at a photograph album. Photocopies of the drawings — the 'photos' in David's album — can be coloured by children and displayed.

The story of David begins in 1 Samuel 16 and ends in 1 Kings 2 in the Old Testament of the Bible.

LIFE APPLICATION

The themes raised here deal with a variety of issues, both inside and outside the family: bullying, friendship, helping each other, and dealing with really serious incidents. They may be used as a series or taken separately.

The fact that David had more than one wife may be helpful to children where there has a been a divorce or a remarriage. This may release them to feel more accepted.

The true story of the horse that had to be put down in the fourth assembly will enable the children to feel righteous indignation without feeling personally upset. This assembly could be linked with the work of the RSPCA. A visit might be arranged or information sent for.

LIVING IN FAMILIES 1
DEALING WITH BULLIES

STORY: KING DAVID'S PHOTO ALBUM

King David flicked through his family photo album and
thought of his many adventures. He had been king for forty
years, and was too old now to lead his people into battle. In
fact he was too weary even to play his much-loved harp. He smiled: there was
a picture of his Dad and his brothers, taken the day the boys joined the army.
That brought back memories. It was because his brothers were in the army that
David had come face to face with Goliath!

Another picture hovered in his head: the giant Philistine standing on the hill
and bellowing to the Israelites, 'Why have you taken positions for battle? I am
a Philistine, and you are Saul's servants! Choose a man and send him to fight
me. If he can fight and kill me, we will become your slaves. But if I defeat and
kill him, you will become our slaves.'

Open-mouthed, David had listened, waiting for one of the Israelites to step
forward and accept the challenge. It might even be one of his brothers! David
had seven older brothers and three of them were soldiers in the army. That was
why he had come. Their father had sent him with some food for the soldiers,
and to get news of the three boys.

But no-one had stepped forward. No-one dared. 'What will be the reward for
the man who kills this Philistine?' David had asked some of the soldiers.
'Someone ought to do it. Who does he think he is, speaking about the armies of
the living God like that?'

'And who do you think you are?' said an angry voice behind him. It was Eliab, David's oldest brother. 'You should be at home, looking after the sheep. You're just a lazy, stuck-up good-for-nothing.'

'Oh no,' thought David. 'I'm getting picked on again. It's not fair, being the youngest. Everyone picks on me.'

Old King David went on with his memories: how he had volunteered to fight Goliath and been taken to see King Saul. It made him laugh to think of it now. Fancy a teenage boy who knew nothing about being a soldier daring to fight Goliath! But he had fought lions and bears in the fields, looking after the sheep. And he was as sure as he could be that God was with him.

And he laughed even more thinking about how he had tried on the king's armour. It was far too big! He couldn't possibly wear that, or use a great big sword. He would just have to rely on his own simple skills, the things he had learned looking after the sheep.

He had made his way down into the valley, stopping to pick up some smooth stones from the stream at the bottom. Then there he was: that great ugly Philistine, shouting and swearing at him. One blow from his massive sword would have cut David clean in half. But there was no need to get that close. All it needed was one stone in his sling, carefully chosen. Then swing it round and round his head, faster and faster. Take aim . . . let go! Pow! Right between the Philistine's eyes! He fell to the ground as if he had been struck by lightning.

There was stunned silence. All the soldiers in both camps were shocked. But nobody was more surprised than David's brother, Eliab. He would have to stop picking on David, now. His little brother had just become the biggest hero in the land!

TALK ABOUT

1. Do you get picked on sometimes?

2. As you walk to school or play in the playground, is there someone you are afraid of?

3. Make up three rules or guidelines for dealing with bullies you might meet.

THINK ABOUT

David put his trust in God and in his own simple skills, the things he had learned at home. You might put your trust in God, or strong adults. You can use your own simple skills, like watching what is going on and talking to adults about it.

LIVING IN FAMILIES 2

A GOOD FRIEND

RESOURCES

- copies of the 'photo' of Jonathan to colour and display. Photocopiable material is on page 201.

STORY: A GOOD FRIEND

What a friend he had been! David eased his aching body up to reach the golden goblet filled with wine. He looked again at Jonathan's portrait. Right from their first meeting, he and Jonathan had been friends.

And how David had needed a friend! It was the first time he had been away from his family. Although his older brothers picked on him sometimes, at least they were around to help him when he needed it. Here, at the palace, he felt all alone.

That was after he defeated Goliath and became a national hero. King Saul had taken him to live at the palace, and used to get David to play his harp and sing some of his songs. But David felt really out of place — a shepherd boy in a palace! It was surprising that Jonathan had made friends with him. Jonathan was the son of the king, a prince. But there had been an understanding right from the start, a readiness to help one another. Jonathan had even given David an outfit of clothes and his sword and bow as a sign of friendship.

As well as the good times, there had been bad times. As David remembered, his face clouded at the thought of the change which had come over King Saul: his jealousy of David because he was a hero. One day, in a temper, Saul had thrown his spear and David had had to run away. But Jonathan had stood by him, even against his father.

At first Jonathan hadn't believed that the king wanted to harm his friend but eventually he could see that Saul's jealousy had changed his father. They had talked for a long time to try to sort out how to protect David. He remembered Jonathan saying, 'Whatever you want me to do, I'll do for you.'

Jonathan had been so worried. They had agreed always to show kindness to each other and their families no matter what happened. There was a party coming up, and David ought to be there. But was it safe? Jonathan said he would make some excuse for David and see how his father took it. David would hide in a nearby field to wait for a signal from Jonathan. At the party, King Saul had flown into a rage, threatening to kill David. Sadly Jonathan had left and signalled to David by shooting three arrows to the far side of the rock where David was hiding. The two friends had met and wept their goodbyes, for they were not to meet again. Some years later, Jonathan died in a battle against the Philistines, fighting alongside his father Saul.

David sighed. What a loss! Never had he known such a friend as Jonathan. Much later he had found Jonathan's son and given him back his lands, so keeping the promise he had made to Jonathan to be good to his family no matter what happened.

TALK/THINK ABOUT

1. Do you have a special friend?

2. Why is that friend so special?

3. Being friends with our own brothers and sisters is sometimes the hardest. Can you be a good, kind and helpful friend to them as well?

LIVING IN FAMILIES 3

HELP FROM THE FAMILY

STORY: DAVID AND HIS WIVES

In the time of David, kings had many wives, and families were bigger than those of today. People lived in big groups, which was useful in providing protection against enemies, for working in the fields, and for collecting water. The children's job was often looking after the animals, as David had done as a boy. If you go to Israel today, you can still see Bedouin children looking after small herds of sheep and goats in the hills.

This is the story of David and two of his wives.

David sighed as he looked at his family photos. He had had some good wives and many lovely children.

His first wife, Michal, was a princess, the daughter of King Saul. Once she had helped him escape from her father. While he climbed out of the window, she put a statue in his bed to make it look as if he was still asleep. It had given him time to get away from the soldiers. But later Michal had hurt him by laughing at him as he had danced in the streets. Michal had never understood that David loved God and that sometimes he got so excited worshipping God that he leaped and danced with delight.

Abigail was different. She had always been so practical. They had met after her husband had refused to give David and his followers food. How ungrateful, when David and his men had protected them against the Philistine raiders! Abigail had been annoyed with her husband, so she had ordered donkeys to be loaded with supplies: 200 loaves of bread, five sheep, 100 raisin cakes, 200 fig cakes, some flour, and two barrels of wine. Without asking her husband's permission, Abigail and her servants took the food to David to say thank you that he and his men had protected the shepherds. Later her husband died, and David had married her.

TALK/THINK ABOUT

1. Has anyone in your family helped you get out of trouble, like Michal helped David?

2. Who is practical like Abigail in your family?

3. What sort of person are you in your family? Helpful, untidy, noisy, kind, clean, interfering, fair, lazy, bossy, happy?

LIVING IN FAMILIES 4
DAVID'S TERRIBLE CRIME

RESOURCES

• copies of the 'photo' of Uriah the soldier to colour and display. Photocopiable material is on page 204.

STORY: DAVID'S TERRIBLE CRIME

As David turned to the last picture he searched the faces, yet dreading to find him. His old eyes peered at each soldier. Which one was he? David would never forget him, although he had tried many times. He was so ashamed of himself.

The Philistines had been fighting the Israelites for as long as he could remember. At first, David had led his armies himself, but as the years went by and his duties as king became heavier, other generals had taken over. Many soldiers had died, but David knew that he had sent this one to his death on purpose.

Ah! There he was! David's bony fingers stopped. Uriah the Hittite. How could he have done such a thing? He remembered sending a message to the general to put Uriah at the front of the battle line so that he would surely be killed. The horrible memory struck him again: how could he?

But even as he thought that, he knew deep in his heart that it was because he had loved Uriah's wife and wanted her for his own. How sad it was that he had sent this man to certain death and angered God. David shook his head.

David wondered if he could be as generous as God had been to him. He had married Uriah's wife, Bathsheba, and they had a baby. But the baby died. Then the shame of what he had done hit David. He lay on the floor and wept. Could he ever make up for it? No, that was impossible. Could God ever forgive him?

60

Slowly the truth dawned. Yes, God could forgive even that terrible crime. Later, they had another baby, Solomon, who was to be a mighty king himself.

TALK/THINK ABOUT

Have you ever done something which you felt really, really sorry for after?

A TRUE STORY TO THINK ABOUT

Gary's granny gave him a bow and arrows for his ninth birthday. He was only allowed to play with them in the garden, but he was quickly bored as he wanted to see the arrows fly a long way. His garden was too small, so after school the next day he hid the bow and arrows under his coat. He shouted to his mum, 'I'm just going out to play!' Before she could ask any awkward questions, he slipped out of the gate and ran up to the field.

'Hi Gary! What have you got there?' His mate, Chris, was already sitting on the five-barred gate leading to the stables. Gary passed the bow to Chris as he climbed up. 'My Gran gave them to me for my birthday.'

'Hey!' Chris twanged the bowstring. 'Here, let me show you.' Gary took the bow and arrows and showed Chris how to shoot. The boys played, each jumping down in turn to collect the arrows. The horses in the field were used to children and galloped freely, unafraid of the little sticks the boys were shooting. Neither the boys not the horses thought there was any danger. But Gary's shooting was quite powerful, and an arrow pierced the eye of one of the horses. Gary ran home upset and crying. He had done a dreadful thing. The horse had to be put down.

TALK ABOUT

1. Gary did a few things wrong. What were they?

2. Dreadful things like that don't happen very often, but if they do, what should we do?

BUNNY BITES BACK!
STORIES OF TWO UNDERDOGS

OUTLINE

➤ The story of a rabbit who terrified a rottweiler
➤ The story of Jonathan and his companion turning the tables on the Philistines
➤ Talk/think about risk, bravery, and trust.

No preparation or resources are needed.

STORY 1: ROGER THE RABBIT

Which do you think cause more injuries that need hospital treatment — hamsters and rabbits, or cows and bulls? The answer is: hamsters and rabbits. Four times as many people have to go to hospital injured by these small pets than people injured by the large farm animals.

One five-month-old rabbit called Roger got into the news by terrorising a Rottweiler dog. Rottweilers have a reputation for being fierce, but four-year-old Beau was terrified by Roger the rabbit. He kept creeping up behind the dog and biting her on the bottom!

Their owner described one particularly nasty attack. 'Roger sidled up to her and just sank his huge teeth into her rump. The next thing I knew, Beau was two feet in the air and howling. She would not turn on Roger because, quite frankly, she is a coward.'

Lots of us like it when the underdog — the weaker person or sports team — comes out on top. Perhaps now we should call them under-rabbits rather than underdogs!

The Bible story of David and Goliath is popular because it doesn't look as if

62

teenager David could possibly beat the huge soldier Goliath. But he does. There is a much less well-known story about David's best friend, Jonathan. This is another underdog — or under-rabbit — story.

STORY 2: TWO MEN SCARE OFF AN ARMY

This happened in the days of the first king of Israel, King Saul. The Israelites had been beaten by their enemies, the Philistines, and the Philistines had done something clever to stop them fighting back. They had got rid of all the blacksmiths in Israel. This meant the Israelites had to go to Philistine black-smiths to get their ploughs and axes sharpened, and they were charged high prices. But worse, there was no-one to make any swords or spears. King Saul and his son Jonathan were the only ones in Israel who had any proper weapons.

One day, Jonathan was with his father and a small army of about 600 men. As they had no weapons, they couldn't do much, so they were just sitting around. Jonathan got fed up. He said to the soldier who carried his armour for him, 'Let's slip away quietly and see what is happening in the Philistine camp.' Off they went, and no-one saw them go.

On the way, they had to go through a narrow valley with cliffs on either side. The Philistines had set up a lookout post on one of the cliffs. When they got near it, Jonathan said to his armour-carrier, 'Let's sort this lot out. Perhaps God will help us. It doesn't matter whether we are a big army or just the two of us. Nothing can stop God giving us the victory.'

'Go on then,' said the soldier, 'I'll stick with you.'

'This is what we'll do,' said Jonathan. 'We'll go out in the open where they can see us. Then if they shout that they are coming to get us, we'll stay and wait for them. But if they dare us to climb up to them, we'll do that. Whatever they say, we'll take that as God's orders for us.'

So the two men stepped out where they could be see. 'Look!' shouted a Philistine guard, 'The Israelites are crawling out of their holes. Come up here and we'll teach you a lesson!'

Jonathan and his companion started to climb up the cliff. The Philistines came at them in ones and twos and they were always able to beat them. All twenty Philistines on guard duty were dealt with!

At the end of the valley, The Philistines in the camp could see their men being defeated. They began to panic. At the same time, Saul had discovered that Jonathan was gone and had set off with his 600 men. They arrived just in time to see what was happening and join in. As the Philistines started to run away, other Israelites who had been hiding in the mountains came out and helped give chase. By the end of the day, the Philistines had been completely defeated.

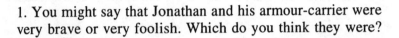

TALK/THINK ABOUT

1. You might say that Jonathan and his armour-carrier were very brave or very foolish. Which do you think they were?

2. They put themselves in a very risky situation. Do you think they were right to trust in God?

SOLVING PROBLEMS

THE STORY OF ESTHER

OUTLINE PLAN FOR FOUR ASSEMBLIES

1. THE KING'S PROBLEM

➤ A group makes visual aids and presents them during the story
➤ Introductory puzzle
➤ The story of King Xerxes' problem for the teacher to read
➤ Questions on the story.

2. MORDECAI'S PROBLEM

➤ The story of the plot to kill the Jews
➤ Script writers — a problem solving activity.

3. ESTHER'S SOLUTION

➤ Esther's problem
➤ Play for a group to prepare: *Esther's solution*
➤ Talk about finding solutions.

4. THE LOST T-SHIRT

➤ Dramatised common classroom situation, with parts for pupils to read
➤ Talk about ideas to solve this and similar problems.

BACKGROUND

The story of Esther is found in the book of the same name in the Old Testament. It is a favourite among Jews, who read it during the Feast of Purim celebrated in late February or early March. Its tale of persecution, in this case narrowly averted, has many echoes for modern Jews. The word Purim means 'lots', referring to the lots that were thrown to decide the day of the mass execution of the Jews. The story takes place in Persia, where the Jews were in exile, during the reign of King Xerxes (sometimes called Ahasuerus) 485–465 BCE. The contemporary Greek historian Herodotus paints him as a cruel and sensual man, very much the impression we get from the book of Esther.

LIFE APPLICATION

The book of Esther introduces us to a number of people who face problems and find solutions to those problems. For the Jews in the story this is a matter of life and death. The children are invited to interact with the story and in doing so to discover some helpful principles in problem-solving which can be applied in school or in their own lives. Four stages in problem-solving are suggested:

1. Understanding the problem

2. Brain-storming, or thinking of different possible approaches

3. Trying the most likely approach to see if it brings a solution

4. Reflection and evaluation.

The first three assemblies each focus on one character in the story and his or her problem. Pupils are encouraged to think about the successive steps in solving problems as they consider each character's dilemma. The fourth assembly exercises the skills learned by considering a common school problem.

SOLVING PROBLEMS 1

THE KING'S PROBLEM

RESOURCES

- photocopies of the instructions and the story for a group to prepare
- catalogues or magazines with pictures of beautiful girls, ladies' fashion and jewellery
- glue, scissors, large sheets of paper or wallpaper
- hardbacked books
- card to make two crowns
- the dressing-up box.

GETTING READY

A group of pupils is needed to help illustrate the first part of the story of *The beauty queen and the three problems*. They will need to find or make some stage props and prepare some illustrations.

One or two people will also need to practise walking with a book on their heads, and miming putting on make-up. Photocopiable instructions are on pages 205 and 206

INTRODUCTORY ACTIVITY

Show the pupils this simple match problem. Draw it on a board. the matches form three squares, like this:

The problem is to take away one match, then move two others — and leave just one. Get volunteers to suggest an answer to the problem. This is it:

That problem is just a simple trick. Real life problems can be a lot more tricky than that. We are going to hear a story in which three people had problems. As we think about their problems, we are going to become better problem-solvers ourselves.

STORY: THE BEAUTY QUEEN AND THE THREE PROBLEMS

Read, or have a pupil read, the first part of the story.

Chapter One: The King's Problem

It was the biggest party any of the guests had ever been to. But then, King Xerxes was the most powerful king anyone could remember. His kingdom of Persia stretched from North Africa to India.

The royal palace gardens in Susa were richly decorated for the party. Every guest had his own gold goblet and the servants were instructed to give everyone a choice of the best wines, as much as they wanted.

The party lasted a whole week. On the last day King Xerxes decided he wanted to show off his wife, the beautiful Queen Vashti. The queen was holding her own party for the women inside the palace, so the king sent seven servants to fetch her.

A few minutes later the servants returned — alone. Queen Vashti had refused to come! The king was thunderstruck. No-one ever refused his orders. He went purple with rage.

All his advisors were upset, too. Each one was used to being the boss in his own house and to having his wife do what he asked. If the queen refused to come when the king called, what might their own wives do? They decided there was only one thing for it: Queen Vashti must be banished, never to enter the king's presence again.

Now the king had a problem. He needed a new queen.

STOP AND THINK

If you were King Xerxes, how would you solve the problem of finding a new queen? Think about the situation:

➤ You are worried that the noble ladies of the court might follow Vashti's example. You want a queen you can be sure will do what you say.

➤ You rule over a vast kingdom with millions of subjects.

➤ You are very powerful and people have to obey you.

➤ But you can't just go out on your own to meet somebody; kings don't do that.

THE STORY CONTINUED

What do you think King Xerxes did? Well, he decided to hold a kind of beauty contest.

Get the group who have prepared the visual aids to come in at the right moments.

Teacher's Words	Pupils' Actions	
He sent throughout his empire for the most beautiful girls to come to his palace so that he might choose one of them as the new queen.	*Show pictures of beautiful girls.*	
Each one was trained to walk properly.	*Walk with book on head.*	
Each one was taught to put on make-up and given sweet-smelling perfume.	*Mime putting on make-up.*	
Each one could choose the clothes to wear and jewellery to make herself even more beautiful.	*Show pictures of clothes and jewellery.*	
Mmm. It was difficult. 'Which	*Show pictures of girls again.*	

one?' thought King Xerxes. 'Which one shall I choose to be my new queen?' They were all so lovely. But Xerxes needed someone who would not let him down as Queen Vashti had done; a new queen who would not oppose him. He pondered, he spent time with each girl. Finally he chose a girl called Esther.

Esther was a Jew. Her people had been brought to Persia as captives a few years before. But Esther did not tell the king she was Jewish. She kept it a secret.

King Xerxes placed the crown on his new queen's head.

King places crown on girl's head.

It was time for another party, Esther's party. He even declared a holiday for his whole kingdom. He wanted everyone to know he had solved his problem.

TALK ABOUT

We might not like the way King Xerxes and his advisors treated women, but thinking about the problem as he saw it can help us learn about solving problems. The first thing to do when we have a problem is to look at all the facts. Let's try that with this problem.

1. How had King Xerxes got into the situation where he needed a new queen?

2. What worried the king about choosing a new queen?

3. Because he was a powerful king, there were some things he could do and some he couldn't. What were they?

4. Why do you think a king could not just go out of his palace and mix with ordinary people?

5. How did he solve the problem?

6. This happened more than twenty-four centuries ago: would he have been able to solve the problem like that if he was a king today?

SOLVING PROBLEMS 2

MORDECAI'S PROBLEM

RESOURCES

None needed.

STORY: THE BEAUTY QUEEN AND THE THREE PROBLEMS

Chapter Two: Mordecai's problem

(Mordecai — say: more-dek-eye)

He wouldn't. He couldn't. Mordecai shook his head. He would never kneel down to another man. He could only bow down to God; that was the way of all the Jews. They worshipped only one God, no matter whether they were at home in Jerusalem or here in a foreign king's palace.

And that meant that Esther's uncle Mordecai had a problem, a very serious problem. Not only himself, but all his Jewish cousins were in deep trouble. You see, King Xerxes had a new minister, a man called Haman. Haman thought himself so important that everyone must bow down before him (except the king, of course).

But Mordecai couldn't. No matter what the other servants and officials in the palace did, uncle Mordecai could not bow down to Haman, even if he was the king's favourite.

Haman was furious when some of the officials told him that Mordecai was not bowing down as he passed. He went to King Xerxes and told him that the Jews in his empire were not obeying his laws. The only thing to do was to kill the lot of them. Haman even promised the king a great amount of money for the royal treasury if he ordered all the Jews to be killed.

King Xerxes listened and agreed. The order went out all over the empire that on the thirteenth day of the twelfth month every single Jew was to be killed. All the things that belonged to them were to be taken.

Mordecai was shaken to the core. As people did in those days, he tore his clothes and dressed himself in rough cloth. He rubbed ashes onto his face. Then he went out into the city crying loudly. Lots of other Jews were doing the same. What was he to do? Was there any way to save his people?

CLASS ACTIVITY: SCRIPT WRITERS

To help us think about Mordecai's problem we are going to pretend we are TV script-writers. Imagine the chapter we have just heard is one episode of a TV serial. Because we are good script-writers we have made a cliff-hanger ending. Will the Jews be killed? Can Mordecai rescue his people? The viewers will want to watch the next episode to find out what happens. We are going to have a script conference to see if we can come up with a good solution for the next episode.

Of course, our solution must fit in with the story so far. So the first thing to do is to go over the facts as we know them. Let's ask ourselves a few questions to check out the facts.

1. Can the Jews change their mind and bow down to Haman? Why not?

2. How is Mordecai related to Esther? What happened to Esther in Chapter One?

3. Thinking about Chapter One, what sort of person did Xerxes want as his new queen?

4. What was Xerxes like when he was crossed and did not get his own way?

Now we are going on to stage two of the script conference, suggesting possible solutions to the problem. [This can be done as a whole class, or in groups with a reporting back session.] See how many ideas you can come up with. The rules are that anyone can suggest any idea even if it sounds silly. Then others in the group have to think if it fits the facts. Might that idea work? Can we think of any reason why it could not work? Can we change the idea in some way to make it better? Let's see how many solutions we can come up with. Next time we shall find out what actually happened.

To be continued . . .

SOLVING PROBLEMS 3

ESTHER'S SOLUTION

RESOURCES

- photocopies of the instructions and play for a group to prepare in advance
- magazines with pictures of food
- glue, scissors, large sheets of paper or wallpaper
- ruler or similar plus gold or yellow paper to make a sceptre
- crowns (maybe from session two) and dressing-up box.

GETTING READY

A group of pupils is needed to prepare a play called *Esther's solution* for the next class assembly. Photocopiable material is on pages 207 and 208.

STORY: THE BEAUTY QUEEN AND THE THREE PROBLEMS

Recap briefly on the situation at the end of part two and any likely solutions that were proposed for Mordecai's problem. Then continue the story.

Chapter Three: Esther's Problem

Mordecai had been good to his niece, Esther. When her parents had died, uncle Mordecai had taken on the job of bringing her up. Now all her people were in great danger because Mordecai would not bow to Haman, the king's most favoured minister. Mordecai had sent a message to Esther through one of her servants, telling her of the danger.

What was Esther to do? If only she could speak to King Xerxes. But there was a strict law that nobody, not even the queen, could enter the king's presence without being invited. To do so was certain death — unless the king held out his golden sceptre to that person. Esther had not been invited to meet with the king for a whole month now. The next time might be too late.

Esther decided not to eat or drink for three days. She told her uncle to get all the Jews in the city to do the same. Their hunger would remind them to keep praying to God that Esther would find an answer to her problem. How was she going to get to speak to the king without him getting angry? As she felt her own hunger, Esther began to think of something that might just please the king.

Introduce the group who are going to perform the play. This is Esther's solution to the problem, and how it worked out.

PLAY: ESTHER'S SOLUTION

Group presents the play *Esther's solution.*

> (*King Xerxes is sitting on his throne with his sceptre in his hand. Haman is nearby. Queen Esther enters and waits for the king to see her. She is nervous.*)

KING My lady Esther, approach the royal throne. (*Holds out the sceptre. Esther comes, touches the end of it, and bows.*) What is it, Queen Esther? What do you want of me?

ESTHER If it pleases you, my king, I would like to invite you and your chief minister Haman to a banquet.

KING It does please me. Come quickly, Haman, so we can do what Esther asks. (*Haman bows as the king and queen walk out.*)

HAMAN The queen noticed me. She did not invite any of the other ministers. I'm the most important. I must go and tell my wife. (*Haman leaves. One or two servants bring on the food. The king and queen follow, then Haman.*)

KING What a wonderful feast you have prepared for us, Esther. Tell me, what do you want? I will give you as much as half my kingdom.

ESTHER My king, I hope you are pleased with me. If you are, this is what I ask. Let me live, and let my people live, too. I and all my people are going to be killed.

KING What! Who dares do such a thing? Where is he?

ESTHER Our enemy is this wicked Haman! (*Esther points to Haman, who falls on his knees, terrified. The king is very angry.*)

KING Haman! How dare you threaten the queen! I am too angry to think. I am going into the garden to decide what to do. (*The king leaves. Haman crawls to Esther and grabs her around the knees, begging for his life.*)

75

HAMAN   Queen Esther, please spare me! Save me! Please! (*The king comes back in. He thinks Haman is attacking Esther.*)

KING   You villain! Would you even attack the queen in my own palace? Guards! Take this man away. (*The servants come and take Haman away.*)

KING   My lady, it is Haman who will be killed, not you. All your family and your people will be safe. I am going to give you everything Haman owned. And Mordecai will be one of my chief ministers. Come. (*The king and queen leave.*)

CONCLUSION

Mordecai wrote a letter to all the Jews in King Xerxes' empire telling them what had happened. He told them that every year they should have two days of feasting and celebration to remember the time that 'their sadness was turned to joy'. It was also to be a time to give presents to poor people. The Jewish people still remember the story of Esther every year when they celebrate the feast of Purim, just as Mordecai told them to do nearly 2,500 years ago. This feast falls in late February or early March.

TALK ABOUT

When we have tackled a problem, it is a good idea to ask ourselves if our solution worked. Even if it did not work, we might be able to learn something that will help us next time we have a problem. So let's think about Esther's problem and her solution.

1. Do you think Esther remembered what had happened to Queen Vashti?

2. Why would just going to speak to the king not have worked?

3. What fact did she remember about the king that helped her find a solution?

4. Did any of last time's script-writers come up with a similar solution?

SOLVING PROBLEMS 4

THE LOST T-SHIRT

RESOURCES

* photocopies of the scripts for six children to read. Photocopiable material is on pages 209 and 210.

ACTED-OUT STORY: THE LOST T-SHIRT

For this assembly, we apply what we have learnt about solving problems through the story of Esther to an everyday classroom problem. We need six volunteers to read the parts of a narrator, a teacher, and four children. Then we can tell the story of the lost T-shirt.

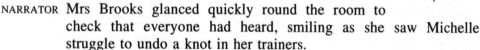

PLAY: PART ONE

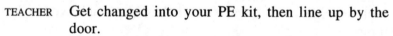

TEACHER	Get changed into your PE kit, then line up by the door.
NARRATOR	Mrs Brooks glanced quickly round the room to check that everyone had heard, smiling as she saw Michelle struggle to undo a knot in her trainers.
CHILD 1	Mrs Brooks, I can't do PE, I've hurt my foot.
CHILD 2	Mrs Brooks, can I go to the toilet?
CHILD 3	Mrs Brooks, my sister borrowed my trainers. Can I go to her class to ask for them?
NARRATOR	Mrs Brooks smiled or nodded in response to each question as she helped Michelle untie the knot.
CHILD 4	Mrs Brooks, I've lost my T-shirt.
NARRATOR	Donna stood in front of her teacher looking tearful. What should she do now?

TALK ABOUT

1. Getting changed for PE can cause lots of little problems. Name some of them.

2. Donna has lost her T-shirt. Let's think of ways to help her solve her problem.

➤ What can Donna do herself?
➤ What can her friends do?
➤ What can her teacher do?

STORY: THE LOST T-SHIRT CONTINUED

Here is a possible end to the story.

PLAY: PART TWO

TEACHER	Does your T-shirt have your name on it, Donna?
CHILD 4	No. But I'd know it if I saw it. It's got a tear in the collar and a red felt-tip pen mark on the back.
TEACHER	Yes, well, having your name on would help. Have you looked in the cloakroom?
CHILD 4	Yes, Miss.
TEACHER	Under the cupboards?
CHILD 4	Yes.
TEACHER	Have you asked your friends if they have seen it?
CHILD 4	Yes.
TEACHER	(*Claps hands*). Quiet a moment, please. Donna has lost her T-shirt. Would you all look in your bags to see if you have picked it up by mistake.
CHILD 2	Donna's friend Charlotte might have it. She borrowed it last week.
TEACHER	Thank you. Now Donna, go and ask Charlotte if she still has it.
NARRATOR	Donna goes out and returns holding a T-shirt and smiling.

TALK ABOUT

We thought about some ways to help Donna find her T-shirt. Is there anything we might put into practice in our class either to stop people losing things or to help them find them?

Perhaps someone could make a poster with guidelines to help solve the lost-property problem.

HOW MUCH DOES GOODNESS WEIGH?

THE KING AND THE WRITING ON THE WALL

OUTLINE FOR THE ASSEMBLY	RESOURCES
➤ Talking about weighing things ➤ The story of the Babylonian King and the writing on the wall ➤ Talk/think about good and bad in the story and in school.	• a balance or scales if you have one to hand. No other preparation or resources are needed.

INTRODUCTION: QUESTIONS ABOUT WEIGHT

Have you used scales to weigh anything recently? (Show classroom scales or balance if you have one.)

Have you stood on the bathroom scales recently? How much does your body weigh?

Have you looked at the label on a tin of beans or tomatoes to find out how much they weigh? (The normal tin size is around 400 grams.)

How much does a tin of goodness weigh? Or a tin of badness? We are going to have a story in which goodness and badness were weighed.

A BIBLE STORY TO READ: THE WRITING ON THE WALL

About 2,500 years ago a message was sent to a king in a city called Babylon to tell him that his goodness had been weighed and his badness had been weighed. Which do you think was the heavier?

It all happened to King Belshazzar when he decided to have a great banquet. He invited a thousand noblemen, and they drank wine from gold and silver goblets which had been stolen from the Temple in Jerusalem, the Jewish holy place, many years before. The party was going extremely well; the king stood up and raised his golden goblet to toast his gods — idols made of gold and stone. But then something really scary happened: a human hand appeared in mid-air and started writing on the wall!

The King's face went white. His knees were knocking and his legs went like jelly. He had to sit down. The guests were baffled. They couldn't read the writing. None of the king's chief ministers could understand it, either. King Belshazzar was growing more and more frightened, his face paler and paler. Then the king's mother came in; she had heard the commotion. She suggested that they send for an old advisor, Daniel, who had helped the king's father.

Belshazzar called for Daniel at once. When he arrived, the king asked him, 'Are you Daniel? Were you one of the captives my father brought from Jerusalem, where these gold goblets come from? My mother says you are very clever and you helped my father. If you can tell me what this writing means, I will make you rich and powerful.'

Daniel told the king that he could read the writing and explain it to him, but he didn't need any reward.

'It is God who sent the hand to write on the wall,' said Daniel, 'and this is how you pronounce the words: Mene [men-eh], mene, tekel, parsin. This is what they mean. Mene: God has counted your days and they are coming to an end. Tekel: You have been weighed on God's scales and found not good enough. Parsin: Your kingdom will be divided between two other nations.'

The king ordered a new suit of special royal clothes for Daniel and a gold chain to go around his neck.

That very same night, the words written by the mysterious hand came true. King Belshazzar was killed by one of his rivals. Babylon had a new king.

TALK/THINK ABOUT

1. Are there any clues in the story as to why King Belshazzar had been found 'not good enough'? (Using the stolen goblets from the Temple; worshipping idols.)

2. What are the good things in our school? . . . And the bad things? . . . If all the good things were weighed next to the bad things, which would be the heaviest?

PART TWO

LEARNING ABOUT LIFE FROM STORIES ABOUT JESUS

A CHILDHOOD TIME-LINE
THE CHILDHOOD OF JESUS

OUTLINE PLAN FOR FOUR ASSEMBLIES

1. A BABY IS COMING!

➤ Introducing the concept of the Time-Line
➤ The beginning of Jesus' Time-Line: before he was born
➤ Think about being important even before we were born.

2. A BABY IS BORN

➤ Chart for a group to prepare comparing the birth of Jesus and a modern baby
➤ Children fill in their own Time-Line label on their birth
➤ A poem to think about.

3. JESUS GETS LOST

➤ A modern story
➤ The story of Jesus at the Temple at twelve years old
➤ Talk about being lost.

4. LEARNING WITH ADULTS

➤ What Jesus' schooling was probably like, with readings for three children
➤ Talk about learning and talking with adults
➤ A prayer
➤ Own school Time-Line labels.

BACKGROUND

The stories of the birth of Jesus can be so familiar from school Nativity plays and Christmas card scenes that we lose sight of the original version as found in the historical documents. It is worth reading them as recorded in Matthew 1 and 2 and Luke 2. Note that there is no mention of either a donkey or a stable; that angels were male and initially fear-inducing; and that the visitors from the east were scholars, not kings.

Due to a miscalculation by a sixth-century monk, the birth of Jesus is almost certainly earlier than that on which the calendar is based. King Herod died in 4 BCE, and a likely date for the birth is 5 BCE. Jesus began his public ministry early in 28 CE and was crucified in April 30 CE.

The only details we have of the childhood of Jesus are given in Luke 2:41–52. The visit to Jerusalem and the Temple when he was twelve years old was likely to be the occasion for his Bar Mitzvah, the Jewish ending-of-childhood rite. This puts into perspective the apparent disregard for the feelings of his parents, who had thought him lost.

LIFE APPLICATION

These assemblies begin to establish Jesus as a human being, with experiences similar to those of children today. They give an opportunity for children to explore their own beginnings, and to see what similarities and what differences there are with a child of another culture.

To assist in this exploration, the device of a Time-Line is used. Labels marking significant events are spaced along a length of wool. Pupils make their own Time-Lines and compare them with a Time-Line for Jesus. A sheet of outline labels is provided for copying on page 211; a group of children might be set to cut them out and punch them ready.

Time-Line examples

Some children, eg those who are adopted or fostered, may have difficulty in the first part of 'A childhood Time-Line.' We must be careful to be supportive and positive. If there are a high proportion of difficulties, it may be better to focus on one or two children in the class as examples, choosing volunteers.

A CHILDHOOD TIME-LINE 1
A BABY IS COMING!

INTRODUCTION TO THE TIME-LINES

We are going to look at the life of a very important person who lived a long time ago. As we look at pictures and read stories, we are going to think about how he was like us and how he was different. I am going to give out pieces of wool (or string) to act as a Time-Line. We are going to tie on to this facts about our own lives in the order they happened. We shall also keep this special one (show larger version) for the special person.

TIME-LINE – THE BIRTH OF JESUS

Who is he? Jesus. You may know the name well, or just know about him as the baby we remember at Christmas. But soon we shall all be experts.

(Give each child their own Time-Line and ask them to stretch it out. Demonstrate with the Jesus Time-Line).

Can you see the label already tied on? That was when Jesus was born. There is a little bit of wool before he was born. Can you see? It's the same on your

87

Time-Line — the birth of Jesus

Time-Lines. Why do you think there is something before you and Jesus were born?

Listen to comments about pregnancy, etc, and answer them simply, only giving as much biological detail as is necessary for the moment. Some of the children's personal comments may have to be followed up privately later.

THE BEGINNING OF JESUS' TIME-LINE

Now let's look at Jesus' Time-Line. Before Jesus was born, his mother Mary had a very exciting, even frightening visitor: an angel! He came to tell her that God was pleased with her and had chosen her to have a very special baby, his Son. As you can imagine, she was upset especially as she and Joseph weren't yet married. She asked the angel about this and he calmed her down, explaining that the baby would be holy, the Son of God.

Mary couldn't really take it all in. Then the angel went on to tell her that her cousin Elizabeth, who was much older than her, was expecting a baby as well. Mary accepted this startling news and the angel disappeared.

I don't suppose an angel came to your Mum to tell her that you were going to be born. Who would your Mum go to see about having a baby? (Doctor/nurse/midwife.) So it was different from Jesus' beginning because no doctor is mentioned in the story. But Mary did do something after the angel had been to see her that your Mum might have done. She went to see her cousin Elizabeth to talk about babies. What sort of things do you think they might have talked about? (names, clothes . . . no nappies in those days!) Some of those things are still the same, and your Mum would have talked to other Mums before you were born. It is an exciting time.

Already Jesus was important to Mary, and you were important to your Mum before you were born.

THINK ABOUT

King David wrote a song in which he said to God

You saw me before I was born and arranged each day of my life before I began to breathe. Every day was recorded in your book (Psalm 139:16, The Living Bible).

David believed he was important to God as well as his mum before he was born. Do you think that is true for you, too?

LOOKING FORWARD TO THE NEXT ASSEMBLY

Explain that we shall really start to use our own Time-Lines next assembly. We shall think then about when we were born. Ask the children to
   a. save the Time-Line carefully
   b. at home, ask *where* they were born, if they don't know already.

A CHILDHOOD TIME-LINE 2
A BABY IS BORN

RESOURCES

- photocopy of the instructions and chart for a group to prepare in advance. Photocopiable materials are on pages 212 and 213.
- the Time-Lines and labels prepared last time.

GETTING READY

A group of pupils is needed to help the class think about the differences between when Jesus was born and a baby being born today. They will use a chart to fill answers to some questions about Jesus and about a baby today. They will need to find Matthew 1:18–2:12; and Luke 2:1–20.

INTRODUCTION

We are going to think about what happens when a baby is born today, and what happened when Jesus was born. A group is going to tell us the information it has found out. Listen carefully, so that you can tell me what is the same and what is different.

(The group which prepared the chart reads the questions and answers for Jesus and a child today).

Questions	Jesus	A child today
1. Who told Mum about the baby?		
2. Where was the baby born?		
3. What transport was used to get Mum there?		
4. When was this?		
5. What clothes did the baby have?		
6. Where was the baby put to sleep?		
7. Who else was there?		
8. What visitors came?		
9. What presents did they bring?		

90

QUESTIONS

1. Jesus was a baby like you were. What was the same?

2. There were some differences. What were they?

3. What do you think Mary remembered that showed that her baby was special?

TIME-LINES

Ask pupils to get out the Time-Lines they were given last time. Show them how to fill in the first label with details of their own date and place of birth. If they forgot to ask where they were born, they can try to remember to do it tonight.

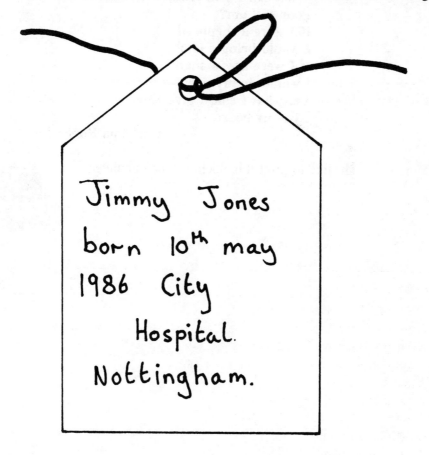

Jimmy Jones
born 10th may
1986 City
Hospital.
Nottingham.

Example Time-Line label

Ask for a volunteer to fill in the label for Jesus with his name, date and place of birth as children give the information. The date is tricky. It can be given as 0 CE. Older pupils might be able to handle the fact that when the date of the birth of Jesus was calculated by a monk in the sixth century, he made a mistake. The most likely date is 5 BCE.

A POEM TO THINK ABOUT

Friends usually bring presents for a baby, like the Wise Men did for Jesus. Here is a poem written by one person who thought about what she could give Jesus as a present:

> **What can I give Him,**
> **Poor as I am?**
> **If I were a shepherd,**
> **I would bring a lamb.**
> **If I were a wise man**
> **I would do my part —**
> **Yet what I can, I give Him,**
> **Give my heart.**
>
> **Christina Rossetti**

Someone might like to print this poem on the computer.

FOR REFERENCE
BIRTH OF JESUS AND MODERN BABY COMPARISON CHART

These are answers for Jesus and suggestions for a modern baby.

Question	Jesus	A child today
1.	Angel	Most probably doctor or midwife
2.	Stable in Bethlehem	Hospital — most children born there these days
3.	Walk or donkey	Ambulance or car
4.	0 CE or AD 0	
5.	Swaddling clothes (like blanket)	Nightie or Babygro
6.	Manger	Probably cot
7.	Animals, Joseph	Nurse, doctor, Dad
8.	Shepherds, wise men	Grandparents, etc
9.	Gold, frankincense, myrrh	Talcum powder, baby clothes

A CHILDHOOD TIME-LINE 3
JESUS GETS LOST

RESOURCES

+ another Time-Line label for each child.
➤ The Bible story can be found in Luke 2:41–51.

A STORY TO READ: THE CUCKOO-SPIT BOY

The children raced on to the playground, each making a beeline
for their own interests. The leaders were treating the children to
a morning in the park. They glanced around; some were on the
roundabout, others shouting for attention on the swings, a few chased a
football over the grass. One boy seemed strangely occupied, moving slowly
along the hedge. This was Luke, intently inspecting each leaf, each twig, in
search of his great love: insects. Carefully he collected leaves covered in the
white bubbles of cuckoo-spit. He was lost in a world inhabited by his tiny
friends.

The whistle blew; the leaders shouted that it was time to go back to meet their
parents. Reluctantly the children left the swings and the roundabout, picked up
the football and trudged back. But not Luke; he didn't seem to hear human
voices.

The leaders checked their group, realising quickly that someone was missing:
Luke. One of them turned to see him still at the hedge, hands now full of leaves
with cuckoo-spit on. Gently she touched his shoulder, 'Luke! It's time to go.'

'Little creatures live in here, Miss.'

'Yes I know. Here. Put them in this sandwich box. Let's go back now.'

JESUS AT THE TEMPLE

Often we enjoy something so much that we do not hear anyone talking to us. It may be playing football or watching a TV programme. For Jesus it was finding out about God. When he was twelve years old, he went with his family to Jerusalem to the Temple. While he was there he listened to the rabbis (teachers) and asked lots of questions. He forgot about everything but what he was learning. His family left Jerusalem and made their way back home. His mum and dad didn't realise that Jesus wasn't with them. They thought he was with his uncles and aunts in another part of the group of travellers. Not until the evening did they return to Jerusalem to look for their missing son.

Being lost is a terrible feeling, isn't it. You feel sick inside as your eyes search

Sample 'lost' label for Time-Lines.

for something you remember, perhaps your blue car or your mum's red dress. Jesus wasn't feeling like that. He wasn't lost, because his mind was in a world he loved, learning about God.

Happily, his mum and dad found him. Jesus was surprised that they hadn't realised that he would be in the Temple finding out more about God. The story ends by telling us that Jesus grew tall and wise.

TALK ABOUT

Who has ever been so interested in something that they did not realise their parents or friends had gone without them? What did it feel like when you found out?

TIME-LINES

Add a label to Jesus' Time-Line saying: Jesus went to Jerusalem when he was twelve. His mum and dad thought he was lost.

If pupils have been lost, they can take a label and tie it to their own Time-Line with details on it such as those here.

Sample 'lost' label for Time-Lines.

A CHILDHOOD TIME-LINE 4

LEARNING WITH ADULTS

RESOURCES

+ photocopies of the quotations below for three readers. Photocopiable materials are on page 214.
+ more Time-Line labels.

JESUS AT SCHOOL

When he was twelve years old, Jesus came to the Temple with his parents. That was the time he nearly got lost. The Bible tells us that Jesus 'was sitting in the Temple with the religious teachers, listening to them and asking them questions. All who heard him were amazed at his understanding and wise answers.' (Luke 2:46–47)

Although the Bible does not tell us, we can be sure Jesus went to school as a boy. School in those days was in the Jewish religious building, the synagogue. The teacher was called a rabbi. The word synagogue means, 'the house of the book'. The book was what Christians call the Old Testament part of the Bible. Jesus learned lots of this by heart, just as Muslim boys learn the Koran by heart today.

One of the things Jesus would have learned at school and at home was the Ten Commandments. The Ten Commandments are God's rules to help us live good lives. Do you know them? Listen to some people reading them for us.

READER 1 I am the Lord your God. You must not have any other gods except me.
You must not make for yourselves any idols.
You must not use the name of the Lord your God thoughtlessly.

READER 2 You may work and get everything done during six days each week. But the seventh day is a day of rest to honour the Lord your God.

> Honour your father and your mother.
> You must not murder anyone.

READER 3 Be faithful to the one you marry.[1]

> You must not steal.
> You must not tell lies about your neighbour in court.
> You must not want to take anything that belongs to your neighbour.

(Condensed from Exodus 20:1–17.)

[1] The Living Bible version.

TALK ABOUT

1. Jesus learned from his parents and the rabbi. Then he was able to talk with the religious teachers at the Temple in Jerusalem. Do you like talking to adults about things you enjoy doing?

2. Do adults listen to you if you ask them questions and tell them things that are important to you?

A PRAYER

This is a prayer about understanding which has been used in schools for over 400 years. You can listen to it, and if you want to make it your own prayer you can say 'Amen' at the end.

> God be in my head
> And in my understanding
> God be in my eyes
> And in my looking
> God be in my mouth
> And in my speaking
> God be in my heart
> And in my thinking
> God be at my end
> And at my departing

TIME-LINES

Labels can be added to both the children's and Jesus' Time-Lines. Encourage the children to put them in the right order.

Example of Time-Line

I Started
School in.......
at ....
My teacher's name
is ....

Example of Time-Line

SPECIAL DAYS
THINGS JESUS DID

OUTLINE PLAN FOR FOUR ASSEMBLIES

---

1. JESUS GOES TO A WEDDING

➢ The story of the wedding at Cana, with a picture for children to look at
➢ Talk about weddings children have been to and what made the wedding at Cana special
➢ Optional Time-Line labels.

2. JESUS HELPS A DISABLED PERSON

➢ A group prepares a model of a Jewish house
➢ The story of the disabled man who was lowered through the roof
➢ Talk/think about being good friends, especially to people who need help
➢ Optional Time-Line labels.

3. JESUS FEEDS A BIG CROWD

➢ A picnic and lunchbox survey chart for a group to fill in
➢ The story of the feeding of the 5,000
➢ Talk/think about helping others, and saying thank you
➢ A prayer of thanks.

4. THE WEATHERMAN'S NIGHTMARE

➢ TV weather forecast script and map of Lake Galilee for a group to prepare. Based on the story of Jesus stilling a storm
➢ Talk/think about being frightened.

BACKGROUND

These assemblies focus on episodes from the early public ministry of Jesus in the region of Galilee. Cana is not far from his family town of Nazareth, and the other three events take place in or near the lakeside town of Capernaum, home of the fishermen disciples. The foundations of what is said to be Simon Peter's house can be seen today in the excavations of Capernaum. A very early tradition records Jesus as having a room in this house. If this tradition is accurate, then this is likely to be the very place where the disabled man was lowered through the roof by his friends. The site of the feeding of the 5,000 is two miles west of Capernaum. Incidental details in these stories reflect accurately the geography and meteorology of the locality.

LIFE APPLICATION

As we look at how Jesus lived his life in ordinary situations (and acted in an extraordinary way), it provides opportunities for children to discuss their own experiences of life. The first assembly will enable some children to talk happily about a family wedding, and all children will know something of the celebrations involved.

The other three assemblies introduce situations of a more testing nature: disability, hunger, fear in a storm, but all are related to children's experience. Ample opportunity should be given for discussion. How we treat others is an important theme here. It may be that some things that arise could be followed up on a one-to-one basis in order to support individual children.

SPECIAL DAYS 1
JESUS GOES TO A WEDDING

RESOURCES

♦ a copy of the wedding scene for each group or a copy on OHP acetate. Photocopiable material is on page 215.

♦ more Time-Line labels if appropriate.

➤ The Bible story can be found in John 2:1–10.

WHO'S BEEN TO A WEDDING?

We don't know about anything Jesus did after he was twelve years old until he was quite grown up and began to do many very exciting things. But he still did lots of the same kind of things we do. There was one time that we know of when he went to a wedding. A wedding is a special time anyway, but this wedding turned out to be extra special.

Give out copies of the picture or show it on an OHP.

The wedding was at a place called Cana, about nine miles north of Nazareth. Can you see Jesus in the picture? He was there with his mother and friends. This was a Jewish wedding celebration and it would have lasted for several days. During this time, the wine ran out and there was nothing to drink. Mary leaned over to ask Jesus to help. Can you see her? Jesus is looking a little upset, for he told her that it wasn't time yet for him to do a miracle. But Mary, like most mothers, took no notice of him and told the servants to do what Jesus said. Can you see the servants?

There were six stone waterpots there and Jesus asked the servants to fill them with water. That was a big job as there were no taps. The water would have to be carried from the well. The servants did that and Jesus told them to pour out some of the water and take it to the man in charge of the wedding reception.

104

Can you see on the picture who that might be? When he tasted the wine he thought it was wonderful, by far the best wine he'd tasted that day. Jesus had changed the water into wine.

John, who wrote down this story, said that this was the first miracle that Jesus did. It made his disciples believe he was someone very special.

TALK ABOUT

1. Who has been to a wedding? Has anyone been a bridesmaid or a page?

Jesus went to a wedding at Cana in Galilee.

Example Time-Line label

105

2. How was the wedding Jesus went to different from a wedding you have been to?

3. What made it an extra special wedding?

TIME-LINES

Children can add a label to their Time-Line if they have been to a wedding. Add a label to Jesus' Time-Line.

I went to the wedding of

....

at ....

....

Example Time-Line label

SPECIAL DAYS 2

JESUS HELPS A DISABLED PERSON

RESOURCES

- a copy of the instructions and illustration for a group to prepare the visual aid in advance
- a cardboard box, scissors, glue, adhesive tape and wool for the group to use
- more labels, if you are continuing the Time-Line.

➤ The Bible story can be found in Mark 2:1–12.

GETTING READY

A group of pupils is needed to make a model of a house like Jesus lived in and some cut-out people. Photocopiable material is on pages 216 and 217.

A STORY: A SPECIAL DAY FOR A DISABLED MAN

Get the group who have made the house and cut-outs ready to show them. Tell the story:

After he left his home in Nazareth, Jesus went to live in a house in a village called Capernaum. The village was near the beautiful Lake Galilee and Jesus had several fishermen friends in the village. The houses in Capernaum looked something like this. (*Ask the group to show their house.*) Can you see that it has a flat roof? It also has thick walls and small windows to keep cool in the hot sun.

He didn't know it yet, but this was going to be a very special day for a disabled man in the village. This man was paralysed; he could not walk. A person like that today would have a wheelchair to get around, but they did not have wheelchairs in those days. All he had was a mat to lie on. (*Ask the group to show the cut-out of the man on the mat.*)

Fortunately, this man had some good friends. These friends had heard about some of the wonderful things Jesus was doing. They wanted to take the

107

disabled man to see Jesus. Because there were no wheelchairs, they each had to pick up a corner of the mat and carry their friend on it. (*Ask the group to show the cut-out friends and to make it look as if they are carrying the disabled man.*)

But when they got to the house, there was a big problem. There were so many people crowding in to see Jesus that it was quite impossible to push through carrying the man on the mat. What could they do? Was it going to be a disappointing day after all? Then one of them saw some fishermen's rope lying outside. (*Show the wool.*) It gave him an idea.

The four friends carefully carried the man on the mat up the stairs and laid him down on the roof. (*Get the group to act this out with their model.*) Then they began pulling up some of the clay tiles and sticks which the roof was made of. Soon they had quite a large hole. Can you imagine what the people inside thought when bits of dirt and sticks and spiders started raining down on them! Just imagine their surprise when the four friends wrapped the rope under the disabled man on his mat and lowered him through the hole right down into the room.

We haven't got cut-outs of all the people inside the house, so we'll have to imagine what happened. The disabled man was lowered into the space where the people had got out of the way of the dirt and spiders. Jesus looked at the man and the faces of his four friends peering through the hole in the roof. Some people might have got angry at the damage and the disturbance, but Jesus was impressed at how far these men were prepared to go to get their disabled friend to see him. They must have believed really strongly that Jesus could help him.

Jesus looked at the disabled man on the mat. Then he said something very surprising. He said that all the wrong things the man had done were forgiven. He must have known that the man felt bad inside about some of the things he had done. But this made some of the other people in the room really angry. They were already cross about getting bits of sticks and clay tiles in their hair, and now Jesus was saying he could do what only God can do, forgive all the wrong a person had done. Who did Jesus think he was?

Jesus knew what they were thinking. He said to them, 'Which is easier: to tell this paralysed man, "Your sins are forgiven", or to tell him, "Stand up. Take your mat and walk"?' Then he turned to the disabled man on the mat and told him exactly that. Immediately the paralysed man stood up. He could walk! He picked up his mat and walked out. He wasn't disabled any more. What a special day! I bet the man and his four friends had the biggest party of their life that night.

TALK/THINK ABOUT

1. What good friends that disabled man had. They didn't give up when they met a problem. How can we be good friends to others who can't do all the things we can do?

2. Do you know anyone who is in a wheelchair? How should we treat him or her?

Example Time-Line label

3. Jesus solved a problem as well. In fact he solved two problems for the disabled man. What were they?

TIME-LINES

If pupils have been ill, or have a friend or relative who has, they could add a label to their Time-Line.

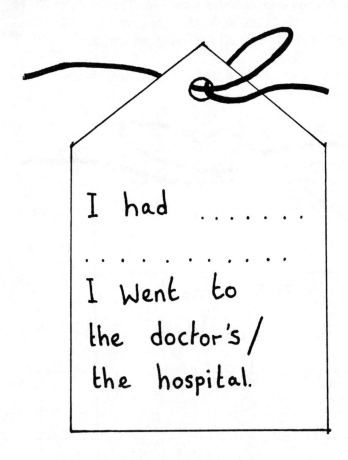

Example Time-Line label

SPECIAL DAYS 3

JESUS FEEDS A BIG CROWD

RESOURCES

• a copy of the instructions and lunchbox survey for a group to prepare in advance
• a Bible

Note. This could also be presented without group preparation. Instead of the survey, ask three children to show the class the contents of their lunchboxes and compare them with the boy's lunch in the story.

➤ The Bible story can be found in John 6:1–15.

GETTING READY

A group of pupils is needed to prepare a survey about lunchboxes, comparing three lunchboxes with what the boy in the Bible had in his. Photocopiable material is on pages 218 and 219.

PICNIC AND LUNCHBOX SURVEY

Get the group to present their Picnic and Lunchbox Survey to the rest of the class.

Owner	Something with bread	Fruit or vegetable	Fish, egg or meat	Food in packets	Other things
1					
2					
3					
The boy in John chapter 6 verse 9					

STORY: A SPECIAL DAY FOR A HUNGRY CROWD

When we get out our lunchboxes it will most likely be a very ordinary lunch. The boy in the Bible had his picnic in a basket because they did not have plastic to make lunchboxes in those days. When he got out his basket it turned out to be the most extraordinary picnic anyone had ever seen.

It happened like this. Many people had gathered to listen to Jesus in a quiet place by Lake Galilee. Some of them had walked miles to get there and almost everyone had eaten any food they had brought with them. Jesus' disciples thought about buying food for them all in the nearby villages, but that would cost as much as one person could earn in eight months. That was impossible. One of the disciples, Andrew, saw a boy come up to them holding out his picnic basket. Who remembers from the survey what it had in it? . . . Yes, five bread rolls and two fish. Perhaps the boy's father was a fisherman in nearby Capernaum.

Most people would not have taken much notice of one small boy and his picnic basket. But Jesus did. He told the disciples to make the people sit down on the grass. There were about five thousand men, as well as women and children. Jesus then took the boy's picnic and said thank you to God for it. His disciples must have wondered what on earth was going on. Here was a great crowd of hungry people and instead of sending them all off to find food, Jesus was making them sit down and wasting time saying thank you for one small picnic!

Then Jesus did something even more strange. He started giving out big pieces of the bread rolls, as much as people wanted. And no matter how much he gave out, there was still plenty for everyone! He did exactly the same with the fish. How would you feel if someone fed a great big crowd of people with the contents of your lunchbox? The boy's eyes must have been popping out of his head.

When they had finished there were so many pieces of bread left that Jesus told his disciples to collect it up so that it would not be wasted. They collected so much that it filled twelve lunchboxes – sorry, twelve *baskets*. That must have been the most special picnic anyone ever had.

TALK/THINK ABOUT

1. The boy gave up his picnic to help others. How have we tried in our school to help other people?

2. Who did Jesus say thank you to for the food? Should we say thank you to God for our food?

A PRAYER OF THANKS

If you want to join in this prayer you can say 'Amen' at the end.

> For tasty snacks and special meals,
>   for savouries and sweets,
> We thank you, Lord, for all good things
>   you've given us to eat.
>
> Amen.

SPECIAL DAYS 4

THE WEATHERMAN'S NIGHTMARE

RESOURCES

- two copies of the script for children to prepare
- a large sheet of paper, felt-pens, Blu-tack, and the map for children to make a large version
- a telephone (toy or cut-out).

➤ The Bible story can be found in Mark 5:35–41.

GETTING READY

A group of pupils is needed to present a play called, *The Weatherman's Nightmare*. Two good readers can prepare the play, and other people can make the weather map and symbols. Photocopiable material is on pages 220 to 222.

INTRODUCTION

Jesus lived for a time in a town called Capernaum by a beautiful lake. Can anyone remember what the lake was called? . . . Lake Galilee. It is so big, fifteen miles long and eight miles wide, that it is often called the Sea of Galilee.
The fish that are caught in the lake used to be famous for miles around.

It is very hilly around the lake. To the east and north-east there are a lot of steep ravines and the wind can suddenly come rushing down these and cause a storm on the lake without much warning.

We are going to hear about one time when a storm blew up that was so violent that even Jesus' fishermen friends were frightened. Whatever happened, this was going to be a day to remember. Let's imagine that they had TV in Jesus' day and that we are just in time for the weather forecast.

PLAY: THE WEATHERMAN'S NIGHTMARE

The Weatherman's Nightmare presented by the group who have prepared it.

WEATHERMAN   Good evening. Here is the local weather forecast for the Galilee area. Well, all is calm over northern Israel tonight, blue skies and plenty of evening sunshine. (*Put on sun shapes.*) That means it will be good for sailing and fishing on the lake tonight.

(*Sound effect: phone ringing.*) Oh! Excuse me . . . yes, speaking . . . are you sure? You are? . . . Alright . . . (*Replace phone.*) I am very sorry, but there has been a sudden change in the weather. Lake Galilee has been hit by a tremendous storm, with very strong winds sweeping in from the north-east and bringing heavy rain. (*Put on cloud shapes and arrows.*) Fisherman are advised NOT to take their boats out as conditions are getting worse. The storm can be expected to reach hurricane strength in . . .

(*Sound effect: phone ringing.*) . . . Oh! please excuse me this is most unusual . . . what? . . . but that can't be right . . . you told me to give a hurricane warning . . . who? He did what? . . . Who is this Jesus? (*Replace phone.*)

. . . er, where was I? . . . oh yes there's been a slight misunderstanding. (*Take off clouds.*) It seems that the storm has disappeared. I can't explain it . . . it just can't happen like that . . . it's incredible . . . I can't cope with this. I'm going to leave it to the Producer to sort out.

PRODUCER: Here is a news flash. A violent storm hit Lake Galilee this evening without warning. Fishermen in a boat on the lake feared they were going to drown. They said they had never been out in a storm like it. The well-known teacher, Jesus of Nazareth, was also in the boat. One of the fishermen described how Jesus just told the storm to be quiet and it died down straight away. Others in the boat confessed that they were really shaken. They said they had never seen anything like it in their lives. That is the end of the news flash.

TALK/THINK ABOUT

1. Have you ever been frightened on a journey?

2. Jesus was asleep in the boat during the storm. His disciples woke him up because they were frightened. Who do you talk to when you are frightened?

STORIES TO MAKE YOU THINK
STORIES JESUS TOLD

OUTLINE PLAN FOR FOUR ASSEMBLIES

1. TROUBLE IN THE FAMILY

➤ Jesus' story of the two brothers
➤ Recap using children's mental pictures
➤ Talk/think about the way the father treated his sons, and does this tell us anything about God?

2. A FARMER COMPLAINS

➤ Two letters for pupils to read based on Jesus' parable of the sower
➤ Talk/think about listening.

3. DINOSAURS ARE PRECIOUS

➤ The story of Mary Anning and her dinosaur bones
➤ Jesus' story of the missing coin
➤ Talk/think about what is treasure?

4. MOTORISTS PASS BY

➤ A modern story of a woman in distress and the people who passed by without stopping to help
➤ A brief look at Jesus' story of the Good Samaritan
➤ Talk/think about why we may fail to help others, and who might help us in trouble.

BACKGROUND

According to our source texts, 'Jesus spoke all these things to the crowd in parables; he did not say anything to them without using a parable.' (Matthew 13:34.) The word parable means 'a comparison'. These comparisons were taken from the everyday life of the people he was talking to. In effect, Jesus was saying, 'You want to know how God views the world and how he wants you to live? Here's a clue: an example from your own experience; now go and think it out for yourself.' There is no need to be a Pharisee or a theologian to

117

understand the kingdom of God; it is mirrored in the everyday world for those with eyes to see. Even a child can understand it.

LIFE APPLICATION

Children may see aspects of their own lives mirrored in these stories. Modern examples help connections to be made. For some children, it will be sufficient for them to reflect on these aspects of their own lives and, hopefully, to gain a little more insight into themselves. Others may be able to take things further and work on what Jesus is saying about God and the kind of lifestyle befitting the kingdom of God.

Topics raised include: how we treat each other both in families and in chance contacts; learning; and the value of individuals.

STORIES TO MAKE YOU THINK 1

TROUBLE IN THE FAMILY

RESOURCES

None needed.

➤ The Bible story can be found in Luke 15:11–32.

STORY: TROUBLE IN THE FAMILY

Jesus often told stories about families. He had brothers and sisters and so understood some of the difficulties. He lived at home until he was 30 – as old as some of your mums and dads – so he would have had a good chance to find out how to get on in a family.

While I tell the story I want you to listen very carefully, and imagine a series of pictures the story gives you, like a cartoon in your head. You can close your eyes, if you like. At the end I shall ask you what sort of pictures you have imagined.

There was a man who had two sons and the younger one wanted to go out and enjoy himself. He asked his father for his share of the family money which he would receive when his dad died. Not a very nice thing to do you might think. It was as if he couldn't wait for his dad to die! Anyway, he went off and did enjoy himself in wild living. It was great – until the money ran out.

By this time he was a long way from home. In fact he hadn't seen his father and his brother since he had left home loaded with the money. So, feeling very hungry, he took the only job he could find: feeding pigs! As he tipped the pea pods into the pigs' trough, he was so hungry he nearly ate their food! He began to think how silly he had been leaving home. Even the men who worked for his father lived better than he was at the moment. He decided to go back and tell his dad that he was sorry for going off like that. He would ask if he could work for his father like a servant. So he started on the long journey back.

119

His father had been worried and had been on the look-out for him. When he saw his son he picked up his long robe, so that he didn't trip up, and ran down the road to meet him. He didn't even care that the village children were laughing at the sight of this undignified man showing his long underpants! He threw his arms around his son.

'I'm sorry, Father,' the young man began, 'I've hurt you. I don't deserve to be your son.' But his father was taking no notice, for already he was telling his servants, 'Get ready to celebrate! Bring the best clothes for my son to wear, a ring for his finger, and new shoes for his feet. Prepare the best food. We are going to have a party! My son was lost and is now found. Hurrah!'

In the meantime the other son came back from working in the fields. He heard the sounds of the party and asked one of the servants what was going on. Instead of being pleased, he was cross, and he didn't want to join in the celebrations. When his Father came to see him he burst out, 'Dad, I've worked hard all these years, I've never complained, and yet he — well, he's wasted all that money on having a good time. Now he comes home and you give him a party. It's just not fair!'

But his dad only said, 'You are always here. Everything I have is yours. We had to celebrate because your brother was lost and is found.'

PICTURES IN YOUR HEAD

Ask the children to talk about a picture in their head from part of the story. See how much of the story can be remembered through different pictures.

TALK/THINK ABOUT

1. Do you agree with how the father treated his sons in the story?

2. Do you think it is easy to be fair in families?

3. Was Jesus trying to tell us something about God in this story? (God is like the father. People may do foolish things, like the younger son, but he is waiting to welcome them back.)

120

STORIES TO MAKE YOU THINK 2
A FARMER COMPLAINS

RESOURCES

- copies of the letters for two good readers to prepare. Photocopiable material is on pages 223 and 224.
- ➤ The Bible story can be found in Mark 4:1–20.

A LETTER OF COMPLAINT

Just imagine that you lived at the time of Jesus and that you weren't going to get anything to eat today unless your family had planted it and harvested it themselves. Farming was a hard job in those days. The soil was rocky and uneven, and most of the work had to be done by hand.

In November, when the first rains came after the long hot summer, the ground was ploughed with the help of one or two oxen. Then wheat or barley was sown by scattering it on the ground. Your job might be to follow your father, dragging a branch to smooth the ground and cover the seed. Harvest time was May or June. You would hope to get a good harvest to make bread to keep you going all through the year. There would not be much time for going to school, so not many people in farming families would have learned to read or write.

But let's imagine for a moment a farmer who can write and who bought some corn last year from a seed merchant. He is not very happy because much less of the seed than he expected has grown and produced a crop to harvest. He decides to write a letter to the seed merchant to complain.

LETTERS

Two pupils read the letters.

121

Reader 1

Korazin,
Galilee

Dear Sir,

I am writing to complain about this year's harvest. My family and I have been working from early morning to late at night, and still we've not had a good harvest. I think it must be your seed. It's just not good enough.

What can a poor farmer do if the seed does not produce good wheat? My family will go hungry this winter with the little harvest which has grown.

Sadly yours,
Reuben, a poor farmer.

Reader 2

Tiberias,
Galilee

Dear farmer Reuben,

I am very sorry that you did not have a good harvest this year. I hope that your family will have enough to eat.

Can I ask you a few questions? Did you look where your seed landed when you were sowing it? Did some land on the path so the birds could see it and swoop down to eat it? Did some seeds land on rocky ground with not much soil so that it soon dried up in the hot sun? Did some of it land in patches of thorns so that it got choked by the weeds?

It is not always the fault of the seed, sometimes there are other things to think about. I am trusting that enough seed did fall on good ground to produce wheat to feed your family in the coming months.

Hopefully yours,
Grobag and Haystack, Seed Merchants

TALK/THINK ABOUT

Jesus told a story about a farmer like the one who wrote the letter. He said the seed the farmer sowed was like things we hear. Sometimes we listen carefully and learn from what we hear. That is like the seed that falls in good ground and produces a good crop. But it is not always like that.

122

Think about school. There are days when we are worried about something that has happened at home, or what someone has said to us. Then we don't pay attention. Does that happen to you sometimes?

Or we might be thinking about that new computer game or the party we are going to. We can be so lost in a daydream that we don't even hear what the teacher says. Does that happen to you sometimes?

The things we don't hear because we are worried or daydreaming are like the seed that gets choked by the weeds or eaten by the birds.

When Jesus told the story, he was talking about hearing God's message, the things God wants to tell people.

The things we might hear in assembly or read in the Bible, do you think these things are as important as other things we learn in school? Less important? More important? Why?

STORIES TO MAKE YOU THINK 3
DINOSAURS ARE PRECIOUS

RESOURCES

◆ pictures or models of dinosaurs

◆ fossils, if available.

➤ The Bible story can be found in Luke 15:8–10.

STORY: MARY'S DINOSAURS

Tell this story. Illustrate with fossils or dinosaur pictures where appropriate.

Mary Anning struggled up the stony beach carrying her basket of curiosities. It had been a good morning for collecting because last night there had been a dreadful storm. The cliff face had crashed in one place, releasing treasure for Mary and her brother.

So what was this treasure that Mary found on Lyme Regis beach at the begining of the last century? Fossils. In fact, Mary didn't know the word 'fossil'. She didn't even know that the strange stones she picked up from the beach were the bones of creatures who had died millions of years ago. All she knew was that elegant men and women travelled down from London by stage coach and paid good money for her curiosities. She made a living by finding them on the beach and brushing and polishing them well.

So whenever the tide was out and the weather was good, Mary would be searching, searching for the special stones. In the years she spent on the beach, she found several different kinds of dinosaur: an icthyosaurus, a plesiosaurus amd a pterosaur. They were sold to museums all over the world, although she saved her best ones for the British Museum of Natural History in London.

ANOTHER STORY: A PRECIOUS COIN

Jesus told a story about a woman searching for something valuable. This woman was not looking for something that had been buried for millions of years, but something that had disappeared just that day. It goes like this:

There was a woman who had ten very precious silver coins that had been given to her on her wedding day. One day, she found to her dismay that one was missing. She lit a lamp and swept the house, searching in every corner until she found it. She was so overjoyed to find it that she called her friends and neighbours to come and share in her happiness.

Jesus said that the angels in heaven get excited like that woman finding her lost wedding present, or like Mary Anning finding the valuable dinosaur bones. But what makes the angels joyful? Angels don't need wedding presents or fossils! Jesus said the angels are happy when someone who has done something wrong turns and says sorry, and really means it.

TALK/THINK ABOUT

1. Most of us keep a few things that are precious to us, our 'treasures'. Who would like to tell us what treasures they have?

2. Christians believe that people are very precious to God. What do you think?

FOLLOW UP

A class treasure table might be set up. Include a photo of the class on it.

STORIES TO MAKE YOU THINK 4
THE DRIVERS WHO PASSED BY

RESOURCES

None needed.

➤ The story of the Good Samaritan is found in Luke 10:25–37.

TRUE STORY: THE DRIVERS WHO PASSED BY

Tell this story:

Barbara stepped carefully along to the Post Office. Her hip
was hurting her today. She wondered if she was well enough to catch the bus
into the town centre? She shook her head. She needed some shopping. She
would have to go, well or not.

Quickly she dropped a letter in the postbox and turned to cross the road. The
road was clear, and Barbara cautiously eased her foot off the curb. She began
stepping slowly across the road. Suddenly she lost her balance and fell to the
ground. Because of her poorly hip, she could not get up on her own. 'Help me!
Please, help me!' she called out.

A car appeared, approaching from her right. Fortunately, the driver saw
Barbara lying in the road in front of him and slowed down. Barbara tried to
smile. The driver would get out and help her to her feet. Then she would be
alright.

But he didn't! He didn't even stop. He drove slowly round her and then picked
up speed and disappeared. Barbara could hardly believe it. Another car came
from the opposite direction, slowed down, and then the same thing happened.

Tears started rolling down her cheeks. A man was standing at the bus-stop
nearby, watching. 'Please help me,' she shouted to the man, 'I can't get up.'
The man hestitated, clearly unsure what to do. But he did nothing.

126

Then two people ran out of the Post Office. 'Barbara! Are you hurt? Let us help you up.' They took an arm each and helped Barbara to her feet, calming her down after her ordeal in the middle of the road.

A SIMILAR STORY JESUS TOLD

That incident happened in an ordinary English town in 1994. It is rather like a story that Jesus told hundreds of years ago. That story is often called 'The Good Samaritan'. Can anyone tell us that story?

Allow pupils to tell the story if they can.

A Jewish man was travelling along a road when some robbers mugged him and left him injured on the road. Two religious leaders came along the road, but they did not stop to help him. Then a man from a country called Samaria arrived. Normally, Jews and Samaritans did not speak to each other. But this Samaritan helped the injured Jew and took him to an inn. He even paid for the man to stay there until he was better.

TALK/THINK ABOUT

1. Why do you think people sometimes won't stop and help someone they see in trouble? (scared? embarrassed? selfish? racist?)

2. What do you think God thinks about:
   Barbara?
   the drivers in the cars and the man at the bus-stop?
   the Samaritan in Jesus' story?

MONEY! MONEY! MONEY!

JESUS AND MONEY

OUTLINE PLAN FOR FOUR ASSEMBLIES

1. THE WIDOW'S GIFT

➤ Looking at foreign coins, now and in Jesus' day
➤ The story of the widow's offering to the Temple treasury
➤ Talk/think about relative values.

2. THE CHEAT

➤ Instant dramatised story of Zaccheus
➤ Thinking about the meaning of the story
➤ Talk/think about cheating, and motivation to change.

3. SHARE WITH ME

➤ A group prepares a simple example of sharing out
➤ Jesus' story of the rich fool
➤ Talk/think about sharing.

4. JESUS AT THE TEMPLE

➤ A Time Traveller's report on Herod's Temple and the commercial sidelines
➤ Some imaginary new school rules
➤ How Jesus cleared the merchants out of the Temple
➤ Talk/think about how ordinary people and the priests felt about Jesus' action.

BACKGROUND

Martin Luther observed, 'There are three conversions necessary: the conversion of the heart, mind, and the purse.'[1] The well-known story of Zaccheus tells of a man whose conversion was complete in Luther's terms, whereas the rich fool in Jesus' story had not even started down the road. Jesus spoke about money more than any other subject apart from the kingdom of God. He did not treat it as a matter of private concern, but deliberately sat and watched the crowd putting their money in the Temple treasury (Mark 12:41). A poor widow's meagre donation occasioned his teaching that the generosity of a gift is not to be measured by its cash value. His direct attack on the potent wealth-generation of trade in the Temple, alongside his exposure of the moral bankruptcy of the ruling priestly class, made an attempt on his life inevitable.

LIFE APPLICATION

These assemblies deal with different aspects of money and our attitudes to it. The first is about giving. Many schools raise money for various charitable ventures, and this might provide a context for talking about the relative values of sums given in the light of Jesus' teaching. Cheating and sharing are covered, and the fourth assembly shows Jesus as a hero, putting his life on the line to confront injustice and greed.

1. Quoted in Richard J. Foster, *Money, Sex & Power* Hodder & Stoughton: London, 1985, p 20.

MONEY! MONEY! MONEY! 1
THE WIDOW'S GIFT

RESOURCES

- any foreign coins the children bring, or some you supply yourself
- if available, a reference book open at a page showing coins from the time of Jesus (eg *The Lion Encyclopedia of the Bible*, p 246) on display for children to look at during the day.

➤ The Bible story can be found in Mark 12:41–44.

GETTING READY

If appropriate to the children in your school, ask if any of them have foreign coins at home and if they could bring one or two to school for the next class assembly. It would be best if they were not very valuable, in case they get lost.

LOOKING AT MONEY

Look at some foreign coins. There might be time to pass one or two round the class. If several pupils have brought coins, they might show them to friends at playtime.

Talk about the shape of the coins, the colour, if they have a head on (a king, queen or president's?), the country of origin, and the value, if known.

In the time of Jesus there was money similar to money today. The coins in Jesus' time were brown, silver and gold coloured — made from bronze, silver and gold. They started off round, but became worn and chipped. Later the edges of the coins were milled, that is, they had ridges to stop people chipping off bits.

In Jesus' time many coins had the face of the Roman Emperor on one side. (That is how we know what the Emperors looked like.) The other side might have a picture or symbol on it, perhaps to record a victory in a battle.

130

STORY: THE WIDOW'S GIFT

There is a story about money in the Bible that happened one day when Jesus was in Jerusalem. It was the week after Palm Sunday, and Jesus was going to the Temple every day to talk to the people there.

One day that week, Jesus was sitting by the collecting-box in the Temple. The rich people were coming up and throwing in lots of money. The money made a noisy clatter when it went into the box. Jesus had seen the big, fine houses the rich people lived in in Jerusalem. He knew they could easily afford what they gave. They were showing off more than being generous.

Then a poor widow came along. She put in two small copper coins. They were only worth a penny. But Jesus called his disciples together to tell them what she had done. He said that she had given more than the rich people had, because she had given all she had to live on. They had given only a small amount from their great riches.

TALK/THINK ABOUT

1. Which do you think is worth more: £100 given to charity by a millionaire or 50p given by a child that was all his or her week's pocket-money?

2. What do you think about people who show off when they are giving money to charity?

MONEY! MONEY! MONEY! 2

THE CHEAT

RESOURCES

♦ two 'cue cards' as follows for a child to hold up:
  'Here is Jesus. He's coming!'
  'That's not fair. He's a cheat.'

➤ The Bible story can be found in Luke 19:1–10.

DRAMATISED STORY: THE CHEAT

Ask for two volunteers, a small child to be Zaccheus and a tall child to be a tree. Position the 'tree', arms outstretched in front of a chair. You will then need two children to hold the cue cards and, possibly, someone to act the part of Jesus.

Tell the children that they are going to help you tell a story. They are the crowds and the 'cue cards' give their words. When these are held up they should say them two or three times to make a babble. Have a practice with these first.

Jesus was going through the town of Jericho near the Dead Sea. Everyone was very excited and wanted to see him. (*Here is Jesus . . .*) There was one man in the town whom nobody liked. His name was Zaccheus. He was too small to see over the heads of the crowd and too scared to push through to the front. So he ran and climbed a sycamore-fig tree. (*Zaccheus stands on chair behind 'tree'.*)

Jesus stopped and told Zaccheus to come down. He was going to go to his house for something to eat! The crowd began to grumble. (*That's not fair . . .*) But Jesus didn't take any notice of the grumbling. He went home with Zaccheus for a meal and a long talk. (*Helpers sit down*)

132

THINKING ABOUT THE STORY

Now why didn't anyone like Zaccheus? There was a clue on the second card
. . . He was a cheat. Zaccheus collected taxes for the Romans, but he cheated
by asking for more money than he should. So, if he was supposed to ask for
five silver coins, he would ask for eight and put the extra ones in his pocket.
People didn't like him, but Jesus chose to go and have a meal with him. Do you
think that is strange?

What difference did that make to Zaccheus? It changed him. The Bible tells us
that Zaccheus said, 'Lord, I give half of my possessions to the poor, and if I
have cheated anybody out of anything, I will pay back *four times* the amount.'
That makes you think. Imagine you took someone's new rubber or felt-tip —
and then decided to put things right by giving back four rubbers or four felt-
tips!

TALK/THINK ABOUT

1. What do you think about cheating?

2. Why didn't people like Zaccheus?

3. The fact that people did not like Zaccheus did not make him change. Why
do you think he did change in the end?

MONEY! MONEY! MONEY! 3

SHARE WITH ME!

RESOURCES

- copies of the instructions for a group to prepare in advance
- the plastic money available in most classrooms
- some of the children's own belongings, eg coats or pencil-case contents.

GETTING READY

A group of three or four pupils is needed to give a simple demonstration in sharing, while the rest of the class guess what they are doing. One person is needed to read a story Jesus told. Photocopiable material is on pages 225 and 226.

INTRODUCTION: MIME

We are going to see three (or four) people doing something simple. Watch quietly, and tell me when they have finished what they were doing.

Ask the group to demonstrate what they have prepared with the belongings and money.

What were they doing? . . . Sharing. There was once a time when Jesus was talking to a crowd, and a man shouted out, 'Tell my brother to share what our Dad left us in his will!' Jesus said, 'It's not my job to sort things out between you. You must do that yourselves.' But then he warned the people in the crowd not to be greedy. He told them the story of a man who was greedy. Listen.

STORY: THE RICH FOOL

A pupil reads the story of the rich fool.

There was a rich man who had some land, which grew a good crop of food. The rich man thought to himself, 'What will I do? I have no place to keep all my crops.' Then he said, 'I know what I will do. I will tear down my barns and build bigger ones! I will put all my grain and other goods together in my new barns. Then I can say to myself, I have enough things stored to last for many years. Rest, eat, drink, and enjoy life!'

But God said to that man, 'Foolish man! Tonight you will die. So who will get those things you have prepared for yourself?'

➤ That story is found in the book of Luke, chapter 12, verses 16 to 20.

TALK/THINK ABOUT

1. When the rich man had a good harvest, what did he do?

2. What do you think he should have done?

3. Jesus said he wasn't going to tell the brothers how to share. They had to do that themselves. Are you good at sharing in your family?

MONEY! MONEY! MONEY! 4

JESUS AT THE TEMPLE

RESOURCES

- a copy of the Time-Traveller's report for a good reader to prepare
- a Time-Traveller's helmet (see details in 'Hearing and Doing 2', on page 194).

➤ The Bible story can be found in Mark 11:12–17.

GETTING READY

A pupil is needed to read the Time-Traveller's report, and make a helmet. Photocopiable material is on pages 227 and 228.

INTRODUCTION: NEW SCHOOL RULES

Just suppose this morning I said that there were some new school rules. Suppose the teachers had had a meeting and that they had decided these rules:

1. No pencils or felt-tips or rubbers can be used in school except those bought at the school shop. This also applies to balls used for games in the playground.

2. No money can be used in school except the new School Dollars. Ordinary British pounds and pence must be changed into School Dollars to pay for dinners or to buy things in the school shop.

And just suppose that when you had changed your pence into School Dollars and bought your felt-tips, you worked out they cost twice as much as in the shops. How would you feel? Angry?

Well, something very like that was happening at the Temple in Jerusalem when Jesus went there on Palm Sunday.

To find out just what was going on there, let's have a Time-Traveller's report.

136

TIME TRAVELLER'S REPORT

- ☒ The year is 30 CE. The month is April.
- ☒ I am in a big crowd of people moving up some steps to an enormous wall. The wall is as high as a twelve-storey block of flats.
- ☒ We go through a great archway in the wall and up lots more steps. The people in the crowd look tired, but excited. Some have come a long way to be here for the festival.
- ☒ At last we come out into the sunshine. We are on top of a platform so big it could hold nearly thirty football pitches.
- ☒ Close to the centre of the platform is the Temple King Herod built. It is covered in gold, and so dazzling in the sunlight that I can hardly look at it. Some of the children who have just come up the steps are open-mouthed in astonishment.
- ☒ Near me is a family who have come from a village in Galilee. They have come to the Temple to offer a sacrifice to God to show how sorry they are for the wrong things they have done.
- ☒ The father is going to buy two pigeons. That is the cheapest sacrifice anyone can offer. He is a poor man, and he hopes he has enough money.
- ☒ First he has to go to a table and change some money. He is not allowed to use the usual Roman money, only the special Temple money.
- ☒ Now he has bought the pigeons from a merchant at another table. They were very expensive.
- ☒ The man and his family go through a gate into a courtyard in front of the Temple. I cannot follow them because I am not a Jew. The mother will stay in the Jewish women's courtyard. Only the man can go through to the inner courtyard and give his sacrifice to the priest.
- ☒ End of report. Returning to my own time.

WHAT JESUS DID

Did you understand what was happening? People were coming to the Temple to get right with God in the way the Jewish Law said. First they had to change some money, if all they had was the normal Roman money. Then they had to buy some pigeons from merchants in the Temple courtyard. The prices were very high. It was just like those new school rules! The money-changers and merchants were getting very rich. When Jesus went to the Temple on Palm Sunday and saw all this, how do you think he felt? . . . Angry!

Does anyone know what he did? (Allow children to tell the story if they know it.)

He went over to the tables of the money-changers and tipped them upside-down! Can you imagine the money rolling all over the place and the fat money-changers trying to chase the silver coins? Then Jesus went to the pigeon-sellers. He knocked their benches over and drove them out of the Temple courtyard. As they went, he shouted to them and to all the crowd who were watching, **'It is written in the Scriptures, "My Temple will be a house where people pray." But you are changing God's house into a hideout for robbers!'**

TALK/THINK ABOUT

1. The ordinary people had already cheered Jesus when he arrived at Jerusalem riding on a donkey. How would you have felt if you had seen Jesus throw the money-changers and merchants out of the Temple courtyard?

2. Do you think Jesus was right to do what he did?

3. What about the rich men in the city, and the most important priests, how do you think they felt about it?

It says in the Bible: 'The leading priests and the teachers of the law heard all this. They began trying to find a way to kill Jesus. They were afraid of him because all the people were amazed at his teaching.' (Mark 11:18)

FRIENDS

JESUS AND HIS FRIENDS

OUTLINE PLAN FOR FOUR ASSEMBLIES

---

1. JESUS CHOOSES HIS FOLLOWERS

➤ A group finds the names of the disciples and thinks about their own choice of people to work with
➤ An event Jesus shared with three of his closest friends
➤ Talk/think about what makes a good friend.

2. THE FRIENDS WHO ARGUED

➤ A group prepares a puppet play about an argument among the disciples
➤ Talk about arguments and how to deal with them.

3. THE FRIEND WHO BETRAYED

➤ A group prepares a play about a police suspect — Judas
➤ Brief outline of the betrayal, trial and crucifixion of Jesus
➤ Talk/think about when friends let us down.

4. THE SPECIAL FRIEND

➤ A story to read. Mary Magdalene thinks about the loss of her best friend, Jesus, and meets him again on Easter morning
➤ Quiet music and thinking time.

BACKGROUND

It was customary among first-century Jews for a teacher or rabbi to gather around him a group of students. Jesus first met some of those who were to become his disciples as followers of John the Baptist (John 1:35–37). Apart from the original chosen twelve disciples (probably symbolic of the twelve tribes of Israel), Jesus also recruited seventy-two others to go ahead of him and prepare the ground (Luke 10:1).

Women were among his followers, too. Luke records three by name who

139

travelled with Jesus and the Twelve, plus 'many others' (Luke 8:1–3). It is highly significant that, at a time when women were considered to be too unreliable to be witnesses in a court case, Jesus chose Mary Magdalene, a woman and a former prostitute, to be the first witness to his resurrection. On the night before his death, Jesus said to his followers, 'I no longer call you servants . . . Instead, I have called you friends.' (John 15:15).

LIFE APPLICATION

Friendship is a vital issue with children, and who is friends with whom is of as much concern in the playground as it is in the early evening soap-operas the children watch. How Jesus chose those he would work with — and who would become his friends — how he dealt with friction and with a friend who betrayed him, these provide models for the children to discuss and compare with their own experiences. The final assembly may be especially relevant to the child who is largely left out, although it is doubtful if this application can be discussed explicitly in the classroom.

FRIENDS 1

JESUS CHOOSES HIS FOLLOWERS

RESOURCES

- copies of the instructions and chart for a group to prepare in advance
- sheets of paper and felt-tips for the group to use.

➤ The Bible story can be found in Luke 6:12–16.

GETTING READY

A group of pupils is needed to prepare a chart of disciples and people they would like to work with. Photocopiable material is on pages 229 and 230.

INTRODUCTION

Jesus spoke to thousands of people about God and what God wanted them to do. However, he knew that he needed a small group of people to learn as much as possible. These people were called disciples. A disciple is a learner or a student. Jesus went into the mountains to pray and then chose twelve disciples. Does anyone know any of their names?

(As children offer names, these can be held up by a member of the group who prepared the list. Those not known are shown by the group at the end).

Some of the group have chosen people whom they could work well with. Let's hear whom they have chosen and why they chose them.

I could work with . . .

Group members talk about their choices and reasons.

Jesus' disciples	People we would like to work with
Simon called Peter Andrew James John Philip Bartholomew Matthew Thomas James son of Alphaeus Simon the Zealot Judas son of James Judas Iscariot	

WORKING FRIENDS

When you work and learn together, you often become good friends. The twelve people Jesus chose started out as disciples, but later Jesus said to them, 'Now I call you friends.' Three of them, Simon Peter, James and John, seem to have been his closest friends. He even had nicknames for them: Jesus called Simon 'Rocky' (Peter means 'rock'), and James and John were called 'Sons of Thunder' — perhaps because they were so noisy!

A shared secret

We share secrets with good friends because we can trust them to be interested. Jesus did that. One day he took Simon 'Rocky' Peter and James and John up into the mountains to pray. As Jesus prayed, the Bible says that his face started to shine, and his clothes became as bright as a flash of lightning. Two men from the past, Elijah and Moses, appeared in glorious splendour talking with Jesus. The three disciples watched and were startled to hear the voice of God say, 'This is my Son, whom I have chosen. Listen to him.'

They did not really understand what was happening, but they knew it was very important. They kept it a secret until later on. They knew they had shared a very special moment with their friend Jesus.

TALK/THINK ABOUT

1. What is it about someone which makes him or her a good friend?

2. Are you a good friend?

3. Are good friends always the best people to work with?

FRIENDS 2

THE FRIENDS WHO ARGUED

RESOURCES

- five copies of the play for a group to prepare in advance and copies of the disciple puppets pictures
- paper, card, scissors, felt-tips, and rulers, sticks or brushes to make the puppets
- a curtain to be held up as a puppet theatre.

➤ Based on the Bible account in Mark 10:35–45 and Luke 9:46–48.

GETTING READY

A group of pupils is needed to prepare a puppet play about an argument. Photocopiable material is on pages 231 to 233.

INTRODUCTION

The disciples saw Jesus heal many people. They heard him say many wise things. They knew that he prayed to God and drew his strength from His Father. They were learning, but that did not mean that they weren't ordinary people who quarelled sometimes and wanted the best for themselves, just like us.

We are going to watch a puppet play about an argument the disciples had and what Jesus did.

PLAY: THE UNFRIENDLY ARGUMENT

Group presents: *The unfriendly argument*
(*Puppets appear 'walking' along the road, (a curtain held up by two children.)*)

JAMES   I was the first disciple. Jesus came up to me and said, 'Follow me'.

JOHN	Yes. James and I had been fishing and we were sorting out the nets.
JUDAS	What are you two talking about?
JAMES	I think us two are the most important disciples. Jesus chose us first.
PETER	No he didn't. Jesus came to me first, before he had even seen you.
JUDAS	But he has given me the most important job. I look after the money, so I'm the most important disciple.
BARTHOLOMEW	But I'm the oldest. I should be given the best place.
JAMES	No, that's for me. Sitting in heaven, on the Lord's right side!
JOHN	And me on the left. Either side of Jesus, our great leader.
PETER	That's not fair. Why should you two be next to Jesus?
JAMES & JOHN	*(Together, loudly)* Because we're the greatest!
BARTHOLOMEW	You two are so noisy! No wonder you're called Sons of Thunder.
JUDAS	Shh! Look, Jesus is watching us.
BARTHOLOMEW	And he's taking a small child and standing him next to himself.
JOHN	What is he doing that for?
PETER	I think I know what he means. I think he's not going to have *any* of us sit near him if we argue like this.
JAMES & JOHN	Oh dear, we've blown it again!
	(Quiet. Puppets walk off.)

TALK ABOUT

1. Even friends fall out and argue about silly things sometimes. Does anyone want to tell us about an argument they had that seemed really silly afterwards?

2. Jesus dealt with this argument just by taking a small child and making him stand beside him. That reminded the disciples of something Jesus had said before: 'The greatest person in the kingdom of heaven is the one who makes himself humble like this child.' That was a clever way of stopping an argument. Can you think of some ways of dealing with arguments?

FRIENDS 3

THE FRIEND WHO BETRAYED JESUS

RESOURCES

- four copies of the instructions and play for a group to prepare in advance
- a sheet of drawing paper.

GETTING READY

A group of pupils is needed to prepare a short play and a photofit picture. Photocopiable materials are on pages 234 and 235.

JUDAS BETRAYS JESUS

Today we are going to have a short play about a friend who stopped being a friend. Imagine a moonlit night in Jerusalem more than nineteen centuries ago. Police Sergeant Solomon and Constable Amos have been ordered to report to the High Priest. The play is called, *The suspect*.

PLAY: THE SUSPECT

The group presents the play: *The suspect*.

SERGEANT   Good evening, sir. Sergeant Solomon and Constable Amos of the Jerusalem Police reporting as ordered.

PRIEST   Thank you, Sergeant. We shall need the services of yourself and a small force of armed men tonight.

SERGEANT   Very good, sir. Is it about this sinister character my men have seen hanging around the Temple? We've been keeping a special watch, what with it being the Passover festival, and there being lots of visitors in town. Tell the High Priest what you saw, Constable.

CONSTABLE   Yes, sir. I observed this man behaving suspiciously in the area of the Temple this evening. We've been keeping an eye on a bunch of trouble-makers this week, and this man is one of them. I'm afraid I lost sight of him for a while. But when I saw him later, he had a large purse on his belt. I'm sure he didn't have that earlier. He could be a thief.

SERGEANT   Very good observation, that, Constable Amos. And talking of good observation, show the High Priest the photofit picture we've had drawn of the suspect.

CONSTABLE   Yes, sir. Here it is, sir. (*Hold up photofit picture.*) It's a very good likeness.

PRIEST   No, no, no! He's not a criminal. He's one of ours. His name is Judas Iscariot. That purse contains thirty pieces of silver I gave him tonight to help us catch the leader of the trouble-makers, Jesus of Nazareth. In fact, I've told him to wait by the Temple courtyard entrance. That's what I want you for, Sergeant. Get a force of armed men. This Judas will lead you to Jesus. I want Jesus arrested and brought here. Quietly. Do you understand?

SERGEANT   Yes, sir. Right away, sir.

PRIEST   And Sergeant Solomon, don't think for yourself. Just obey orders. Now!

THE ARREST

Thank you, High Priest, Sergeant Solomon and Constable Amos. Of course, they did not have policemen and photofit pictures in those days. But they did have a Temple guard. And the bit about Judas being paid thirty silver pieces to lead the armed men to arrest Jesus is true. Who knows what happened next?

See if pupils can briefly outline the story. Judas led the armed men to the Garden of Gethsemane outside the city. He went up to Jesus and gave him a greeting kiss on the cheek. This was a sign to guards. They arrested Jesus and took him to the High Priest's house. He was tried, and then taken to the Roman Governor, Pilate. Jesus was sentenced to death and crucified.

TALK/THINK ABOUT

1. Friends can sometimes let us down, although we hope we never have a friend who betrays us like Judas betrayed Jesus. How does it feel when a friend lets you down?

2. Although his disciples let him down sometimes, Jesus never stopped being friends with them. He always forgave them. If our friend lets us down, should we go on being cross with them, or forgive them and make up?

FRIENDS 4

THE SPECIAL FRIEND

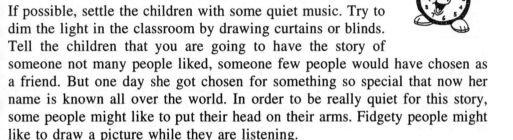

RESOURCES

♦ tape-player and quiet music.

GETTING SETTLED

If possible, settle the children with some quiet music. Try to dim the light in the classroom by drawing curtains or blinds. Tell the children that you are going to have the story of someone not many people liked, someone few people would have chosen as a friend. But one day she got chosen for something so special that now her name is known all over the world. In order to be really quiet for this story, some people might like to put their head on their arms. Fidgety people might like to draw a picture while they are listening.

MARY'S STORY

Mary Magdalene tried to wipe the tears from her cheeks, but they just kept coming. She had never had any real friends her whole life until the last few months, and now the best friend of all was dead. She couldn't believe it: Jesus was dead. And it had all happened so quickly.

Just last Sunday they had arrived in Jerusalem with such excitement. Jesus was riding on a donkey, and crowds of people had come out to cheer and wave branches and even call him a king! Mary had followed behind with Peter and John and the other disciples. These were her new friends. There were some other women as well who followed Jesus. They all accepted Mary and made her one of them, even though some of the snobby people said she was not a nice person.

What a commotion there had been when Jesus went into the Temple and threw

149

over the tables of the money-changers! The ordinary people loved Jesus for that. Mary loved him, too. She loved the way he made people feel wanted and told them that God was their loving Father. The people had flocked to the Temple every day to hear him talk.

Then, on Thursday night, the awful thing had happened. Judas had gone out in the middle of the meal. He had gone to betray Jesus to his enemies! How could anyone do that to Jesus? The guard had come and arrested Jesus later that night in the olive garden. Mary could not even bear to think of what they had done to him after that, the way they had beaten him and crucified him. Now he was dead, laid in a cold rock tomb.

There was only one thing she could do for Jesus now. She would go with the other women as soon as it was light to prepare his body for burial. There had not been time to do it properly when they took him down from the cross. It was the only way she could say goodbye.

As they hurried through the quiet Sunday morning city, the women remembered the great round stone that had been rolled in front of the rock cave tomb. Could they move it themselves? Or would the soldiers who had been posted on guard move it for them? Perhaps the soldiers would not even let them near.

At last they could see the white rock of the cliff through the trees in the garden. But the tomb? It was open! The stone was rolled to the side! The soldiers had gone! Where was Jesus?

Then it was all panic and running. Running back into the city. Hammering on the door. Shouting, 'He's gone! We don't know where they have put him.' Running back to the tomb again with Peter and John. Peter going inside and seeing the cloth Jesus was wrapped in just lying there on its own. Then the men running back to tell the other disciples in the city.

Finally, there was silence. Mary stood alone in the garden by the empty tomb, crying. But she wasn't alone. There was somebody standing quietly close by. Perhaps it was the gardener? He spoke to her: 'Woman, why are you crying? Who is it you are looking for?'

'Sir,' said Mary, her eyes blinded by tears, 'if you have carried him away, tell me where you have put him, and I will get him.'

He only said one word in reply. It was her name: 'Mary'.

Mary! There was no-one in the whole world who spoke her name like that. Only Jesus. Only Jesus! She turned and reached out to hold him. 'Teacher!' It *was* Jesus. Jesus was alive!

She didn't have time to think then, but later she would think. She would say to herself, 'He didn't choose Peter to be the first person to see him alive. He didn't choose James, or John, or any of his other friends. He didn't choose a man at all. He chose me. Mary Magdalene. The one people said was not a nice person. Jesus chose *me* to be his special friend.'

MUSIC

Play some more quiet music, if appropriate, to allow a couple of minutes for reflection.

PART THREE

LIFE'S BIG QUESTIONS

LIFE'S BIG QUESTIONS

The teacher asked to discuss ultimate questions with children faces two possible difficulties. The first is that many of us have little experience of talking about life and death, purpose and God, as such topics are often taboo in British conversation. The second is that part of the role of a teacher is to be the authority who either has the answers or can point to where they may be found. Here, we are dealing with questions which have no easy answers, and which we ourselves may be quite unsure about. The sense of authority may be lacking, and this can be quite unsettling.

On the other hand, we may have thought through these questions and arrived at a clear personal conviction. We shall then be aware of the danger of imposing our own beliefs and of not giving the children space to express their views with confidence. These assemblies provide material for the majority of acts of worship that are required to be broadly Christian. Their aim is to allow children to gain an understanding of Christian perspectives on some ultimate questions, while respecting their right to hold differing views or to reserve their judgement.

Having faced these difficulties, the teacher will be aware that many children have few, if any, opportunities to talk about such questions. Yet 'Who made God?' and 'Why did my rabbit die?' and 'Why am I here?' are commonplace questions in a child's life. Treating such questions seriously and honestly is a significant aid to a child's general development.

There are no Life Application sections for these assemblies, because the very act of thinking about ultimate questions *is* the application. Beyond that, the need for tolerance and for respect for the opinions, beliefs, and doubts of others, which the teacher may want to stress many times, is a vital life application that comes through the process of classroom discussion.

A visual aid to the series is a selection of large jigsaw pieces. These symbolise the fact that we are dealing with matters which are a puzzle, a mystery. There will be missing pieces, too, a recognition that all answers are incomplete. Words or simple drawings on the pieces will remind pupils of the particular questions tackled. A suitable space in the classroom should be found to display them.

ASKING QUESTIONS

INTRODUCING THE SERIES ON 'LIFE'S BIG QUESTIONS'

BACKGROUND

We introduce the series on 'Life's big questions' by thinking about three kinds of questions: easy questions, silly questions, and big questions. There are other kinds of questions, of course, but this classification helps pupils to differentiate between certain kinds of questions and gives them an entry point to a difficult subject. Even here, one person's big question may be another person's silly question. Respect for each other will need to be stressed.

RESOURCES

♦ photocopy of the 'Easy, Silly and Big questions' chart for a group to prepare in advance
♦ some large jigsaw-piece shapes cut from card. Photocopiable material is on pages 236 to 238
♦ noticeboard or other clear area to display jigsaw pieces and questions.

GETTING READY

The group set to prepare the questions chart will need to be one of the more able groups in the class. Alternatively, the teacher could prepare three sets of questions and omit the group work.

THREE KINDS OF QUESTIONS

Introduce the group who have been thinking about different types of questions. Talk about each type of question in turn and get the members of the group to read out their examples.

Can the class think of some more big questions? Sometimes something may be a big question for me, but not for everybody. For example, 'Why did my cat get run over, because that made me very upset?'

Big questions don't have easy answers. If they did, they would be easy questions! The answers to big questions are often like pieces of a jigsaw puzzle. (Display cut-outs.) We have some of the pieces, but we are not sure how they fit together. And it looks as if some of the pieces are missing.

Just to make it even harder, people often disagree about the jigsaw-piece answers to big questions.

Tell the class you are going to use some assemblies to think about some big questions. This will be brain-stretching time! It might be a good moment to talk about listening to each other and respecting other people's views.

If you wish, you could tell the class that the question you are going to think about next time is: Who made God? Is that an easy question, a silly question, or a big question? It could be written on a board with the jigsaw pieces. Leave them to think about it.

FOR REFERENCE: PUPILS' CHART

Easy questions	Silly questions	Big questions
1. What colour is grass?	Where do pineapples lay their eggs?	Did God make the world or did it just happen?
2.		
3.		
4.		

WHO MADE GOD?

BACKGROUND

This is one of the most common of children's questions about God. The concept of the silly question introduced in the previous assembly comes to our aid as we show why this question falls into that category.

However, that only reveals the big question behind it, the question of ultimate origins. Either we believe in a Creator God, or we believe that the universe is a closed system with no supernatural agent, or we say that we honestly don't know.

Once again, respect for each other's views is paramount. It is also important to openly acknowledge that thinking about such questions can make us feel very small and inadequate, even the teacher. That's okay, it's the same for everybody!

RESOURCES

♦ a jigsaw piece with 'SUPER-GOD?' written on it. Photocopiable material is on page 239.

DIFFERENT TYPES OF QUESTIONS

Remind pupils of the last assembly and see if they can remember one or two examples of easy, silly and big questions (or give new ones).

WHO MADE GOD?

People sometimes ask this question; 'Who made God?' Is that an easy question, a silly question, or a big question? Let's try to think about it for a few moments.

Can any of us make anything that is more clever than we are? . . . No. Even the biggest computers can only do what their makers tell them to do. So if someone — or something — made God, he must be more clever than God. So we'll call him 'Super-God'. Does everyone agree with that? (Show the jigsaw piece.)

But wait. Who made Super-God? He must be cleverer than Super-God, so we had better call him something like, 'Mega-Super-God'!

Clearly we could go on asking 'Who made Hyper-Mega-Super-God?' questions for ever. That is just silly. If you try to answer the question 'Who made God?' you get a silly answer. So that means it must be a silly question!

When we talk about 'God', we mean the person or thing who made everything else, but who was not made himself. To ask 'Who made God?' is a silly question. God just is.

Each one of us has a choice. We can believe in this God who just is, who made everything else. Or we can believe that there is no God and that the universe — the world, the stars, space — just is. No-one made it, it just happened. Or we can say, 'I don't know whether there is a God or not. I haven't made up my mind yet. I want to think about it some more.'

TALK ABOUT

Space might be given for pupils who want to, to say whether they believe in God or not, or have not yet made up their minds.

CONCLUSION

In future assemblies we will look at some of the reasons people have for believing in God and what God is like.

DOES GOD EXIST?

BACKGROUND

Does God exist? The classic argument from design was set out in the eighteenth century by William Paley. Paley argued that if you found a watch on the ground while walking across a heath, you would not assume it had always been there, as you might a stone. The watch must have had a maker. The complexity and design evident in nature argue even more strongly in favour of a divine Maker.

This view was challenged by Hume, Darwin and others, and lately by biologist Richard Dawkins in *The Blind Watchmaker*. However, much recent research on both the origins of the universe and the variables needed for life to exist has led to the argument from design being restated with renewed vigour. The basis for this assembly is some of that research.[1]

This assembly starts from pupils' interest in environmental protection and asks a group to design an eco-house. An eco-house is one that is environmentally friendly, uses minimal resources, and recycles waste where possible. The earth is then considered as a giant eco-house, evidence for many people of the existence of a Designer. The section below which considers earth as an eco-house might be edited or expanded depending on the children's knowledge.

RESOURCES

- a copy of the instructions for a group to prepare in advance
- a large sheet of drawing paper
- a globe to display when talking about the Earth
- a jigsaw piece with a sketch of the Earth on it. Photocopiable material is on pages 240 and 241.

GETTING READY

A group of pupils is needed to design a house to live in which will care for the environment.

INTRODUCTION: IDEAS FOR AN ECO-HOUSE

One of life's big questions is, 'Does God exist?' Today we are going to think about one of the reasons some people have for believing that God exists. To help us, we are going to start by looking at a special house designed by one group.

Introduce the concept of the eco-house and get the group to show the picture (if they have drawn one) and talk about their eco-house.

EARTH IS AN ECO-HOUSE

One of the writers in the Bible says this: **'Every house is built by someone, but God is the builder of everything.'** (Hebrews 3:4) 'Every house is built by someone' — that is obviously true. When we see a house we don't imagine it grew out of the ground like a toadstool or happened by accident. Someone drew up the plans for the house and someone built it. An eco-house needs an extra lot of thought going into the plans.

Now think of the Earth. (Show the globe.) The Earth is a like a gigantic eco-house. It has an insulating blanket of air and clouds to keep the warmth in. It has an energy source, the sun, at exactly the right distance to provide heat and light without frying us. Green plants capture some of that energy and store it. It has a protective layer of ozone to keep out harmful radiation. It has an excellent water purifying and recycling system: clean water simply rains down out of the sky for free and all we have to do is catch it. It has whole armies of waste-disposal workers: scavengers, fungi and bacteria. It has an air-purification and oxygen supply system: green plants again. Billions of people and thousands of billions of animals live in this eco-house.

The Bible writer said: 'Every house is built by someone, but God is the builder of everything.' Is God the builder of everything? Does God exist? Some people look at the Earth and say, 'Someone built this. The Earth is a giant eco-house. It did not happen by accident. It was very carefully planned. The planner must be God. I believe God exists.'

TALK/THINK ABOUT

Other people have different ideas. Some say that there are probably billions of planets in the universe and some of those planets must be just right for life to exist on them. What do you think?

1. See for example Hugh Ross, *The Creator And The Cosmos* (Navpress: Colorado, 1993); John Wright, *Designer Universe* (Monarch: Crowborough, 1994).

WHAT IS GOD LIKE? 1

BACKGROUND

How can human beings know what God is like? In his letter to the church at Rome, St Paul proposed that we can know about God's 'invisible qualities' by looking at the universe he has made (Romans 1:20). Jesus pointed the way in his more direct fashion when he told his listeners, 'Look at the flowers . . . Look at the birds . . . '.

Here we introduce the concept of knowing about someone without seeing them first by way of a simple game, then by looking at items in the classroom created by the children themselves. Finally we ask an open-ended question, 'What can we know about God by looking at the things he has created?' Even for those who do not believe in God it is an interesting exercise.

If children have a mental picture of God as a grandad figure with a big white beard, that is fine. Ultimately it may prove to be as close to the truth as the most sophisticated theologian's concept of God!

RESOURCES

+ a jigsaw piece with the question 'What is God like?' written on it. Photocopiable material is on page 242.
+ a variety of items from the classroom that pupils have created themselves, eg painting, poem, technology project
+ a blindfold
+ a picture of stars in an astronomy book

KNOWING WITHOUT SEEING

Today's big question is, 'What is God like?' (Show jigsaw piece.) That is a hard question because we can't see God. To help us think about this question we shall start with a silly game many of us have played at parties. This is: Squeak, piggy, squeak! One person is blindfolded and then someone else is secretly chosen. This person has to sit on the knee of the blindfolded person and make a squeaking noise like a pig. The blindfolded person has to guess who it is.

Play a couple of rounds. Ask the blindfolded child first to say whether the other is a boy or a girl, then to guess their name.

If you can't see, can you usually tell whether the other person is a boy or a girl, a child or a grown-up? . . . We can tell a little about what a person is like from the noise they make, even if we can't see them.

THINGS WE HAVE MADE

Let's look at some other things people have made apart from silly squeaking noises! (Show the chosen items.) Can we tell something about what the person is like from what they have created? Can we guess perhaps their favourite colours, or the things they are interested in, or how much practice they have had making this kind of thing?

THINGS GOD HAS MADE

One of the writers in the Bible said this:

> There are things about God that people cannot see — his eternal power and all the things that make him God. But since the beginning of the world those things have been easy to understand. They are made clear by what God has made (Romans 1:20).

This writer says that even though we cannot see God, we can know what he is like by looking at the things he has made. If God is the Maker of the Earth, our eco-house, then there are millions of things for us to look at that he has made.

TALK/THINK ABOUT

1. Show picture of stars. There are, billions of stars, each one as big or bigger than our sun. If someone believes that God is the Creator, what might the stars tell that person about God? (He is very big, powerful, clever.)

2. Show picture of flowers. How many different kinds of flowers can we think of? . . . What might that tell someone about God? (He loves colour, variety, beauty.)

WHAT IS GOD LIKE? 2

BACKGROUND

In the Old Testament, God was occasionally likened to a father, one metaphor among many. Jesus introduced a radically new concept by calling God 'the Father' and himself 'the Son'. He drew an explicit lesson from this relationship by saying, 'He who has seen me has seen the Father'. In the whole history of religion, no clearer answer has been given to the question, 'What is God like?'

Family likeness is a familiar topic of conversation in most homes and gives us a friendly introduction to a second bite at this big question.

RESOURCES

- perhaps a photo of your own parent or parents
- photos of parents which children bring in
- jigsaw piece with matchstick parent and child. Photocopiable material is on page 243.

GETTING READY

The day before this classroom assembly, ask the children if some of them would like to bring in a photo of a parent or parents to show the rest of the class.

JUST LIKE HER MOTHER!

Look at any photos and talk about how we may look like our parents. Hair or eye-colour may be the same, or build, or nose-shape.

We can be like our parents in other ways, too. Talk about liking the same sorts of food, or being good at the same subjects at school, or enjoying the same sport or hobby. Allow children who want to, to contribute to the discussion.

JUST LIKE HIS FATHER!

Last time we asked the big question, 'What is God like?' We thought about one way of finding out what God is like: by looking at the things he has made.

Wouldn't it be nice if we could also look at a member of his family and say, 'God is just like that'?

Well, Jesus said we could. Jesus nearly always called God, 'the Father'. And he often called himself, 'the Son'.

One day some of Jesus' friends were asking this same big question. One of them, Philip, said to Jesus, 'Lord, show us the Father. That is all we need.'

Jesus answered, 'I have been with you a long time now. Do you still not know me, Philip? He who has seen me has seen the Father' (John 14:8–9).

Jesus was saying, 'If you know what I am like, you know what my Father God is like. Even though you can't see God, you know what *he* is like because you are my friends and you know what *I* am like.'

TALK/THINK ABOUT

1. Did Jesus mean that God the Father looked like him or that he was the same kind of person as himself?

2. What do you think Jesus' friends learned about what God is like by being with Jesus?

WHY AM I HERE? 1

BACKGROUND

'There is substantial evidence that one of the most serious problems amongst today's schoolchildren and students is a sense of meaninglessness, loss of direction and purpose. . . . People do need to know what life is about in order to live effectively when the issues of sheer survival are settled. Nothing will excuse our inability to supply a training to meet that need.' John Peck, *Wisdom In The Marketplace*, (Greenbelt Festivals: London, 1989) p 109.

RESOURCES

+ several school or household objects the purpose of which you can talk about easily, eg pencil-sharpener, pliers, preferably including one more obscure object whose use the children will have to guess at
+ a jigsaw piece with a matchstick person and a question mark on it. Photocopiable material is on page 244.

WHAT IS ITS PURPOSE?

Show your objects one at a time and ask what each one was made for, what is its purpose.

Bring a pupil out to the front and ask what is the purpose of this 'object'? Is it to make a teacher's life a misery?! Or to be a future Prime Minister? Or to make the world's largest collection of baked-bean can labels? Any other ideas?

'What is the purpose of this 'object' — a person?' Is that an easy question, a silly question, or a big question? (Give pupils space to talk about this.)

Hopefully they will reach the conclusion that this is really a big question. One of life's big questions is, Why am I here? What was I made for? What is my purpose in living on planet Earth? Show the jigsaw piece with a matchstick person and question mark.

WHAT PAUL SAID

There is a letter in the Bible which talks about the 'purpose' of a human being, what we are made for. This letter was written by a famous man called Paul. In this letter he said that our bodies are like a tent we live in. Paul was a tent-maker, so he knew a lot about tents. Listen carefully to what Paul said happens when people die, and see if you can answer some questions afterwards.

We know that our body — the tent we live in here on earth — will be destroyed. But when that happens, God will have a house for us to live in. It will not be a house made by men. It will be a home in heaven that will last for ever. . . . This is what God made us for (2 Corinthians 5:1 and 5a).

QUESTIONS

1. What did Paul say our bodies are like? (A tent that we live in here on earth.)

2. After we die, what does Paul say we shall have to live in then? (A 'house'. If our bodies now are like a tent, which can easily get blown down, we shall have new bodies then which will be much stronger, like a house is stronger than a tent.)

3. Where will this 'house' be? (In heaven.)

4. How long will it last? (Forever.)

5. What was the last thing Paul said? ('This is what God made us for.')

So Paul's answer to the question, 'Why am I here?', is that God made people in order that they should live with him in heaven. He made them so that they would have different bodies in heaven, as different as a house is from a tent. And he made them to live with him for ever.

WHY AM I HERE? 2

RESOURCES

- a bag or small suitcase and items you might take on holiday eg swimsuit, sun-lotion, passport, etc.
- a jigsaw piece with a matchstick man and a question mark on it (as for WHY AM I HERE? 1).
- copies of the group preparation sheet
- half-a-dozen sheets of plain A4 paper, scissors, felt-pens.

GETTING READY

Two pupils are needed; one to read 'Peter's list', the other to hold up slips of paper with the words on and drop them in a bag. Photocopiable materials are on pages 245 and 246.

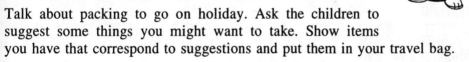

PACK YOUR BAGS

Talk about packing to go on holiday. Ask the children to suggest some things you might want to take. Show items you have that correspond to suggestions and put them in your travel bag.

Show the jigsaw piece from the previous assembly with the matchstick person and question mark. What was the big question? — 'Why am I here?' 'What was I made for?' The answer Paul gave in the Bible was that God made people so that they would live with him in heaven for ever.

If Paul was right, and God made people to live for ever in heaven, how should we get ready for that here on earth? If we could take a bag with us to heaven what would we put in it? We can't take our bodies. Paul said our bodies are just like a tent we live in that is going to get worn out and thrown away. God will give us new bodies.

Could we take money with us? . . . Could we take our bike or favourite computer game? . . . No. Anyway, Paul said there are far more exciting things in heaven, things that are indescribably good. We need to empty the bag: no swimsuits, no passports, no sun-lotion.

So what could we take? How could we get ready? What could we put in our empty one-way-trip-to-heaven bag?

PETER'S LIST

One person who might be able to help us is Peter. Peter was one of Jesus' closest friends. Like Paul, Peter wrote some letters. In one of them he made a list of the kind of things to be getting ready for a trip to heaven.

Introduce the group who are going to read the list.

PETER'S LIST

The first thing Peter said should go in the bag is: faith. That is, trusting in God. Have the word 'faith' displayed and put in the bag. Let the group go through the rest of Peter's list.

BEFORE THE READER
STARTS   faith

READER	WORDS
Try as much as you can to add these things to your lives: to your faith, add goodness;	goodness
and to your goodness, add knowledge;	knowledge
and to your knowledge, add self-control;	self-control
and to your self-control, add the ability to hold on;	being able to hold on
and to your ability to hold on, add service for God;	service for God
and to your service for God, add kindness to your brothers and sisters in Christ;	kindness
and to this kindness, add love.	love

PETER'S ANSWER

Peter went on to say to other Christians, 'If you do all these things, . . . you will be given a very great welcome into the kingdom of our Lord and Saviour Jesus Christ. That kingdom continues for ever.'

In other words, Peter was saying to them: If you have got these things in your bag (show the papers with the words on), God is going to be very pleased to see you and to give you a great big welcome into heaven.

Why am I here? Peter's answer is, 'I'm here to get my trip-to-heaven bag ready.'

TALK/THINK ABOUT

1. Can we buy things like kindness and goodness and self-control? Where do they come from?

2. If people agree with Peter, should they wait until they are older to start getting their trip-to-heaven bag ready, or should they start when they are young?

WHY DO BAD THINGS HAPPEN? 1

BACKGROUND

The problem of suffering is perhaps the biggest question there is. Much as we try to shield children from suffering, many will have already experienced real pain of different kinds. We can't pretend to have a full answer, but we can help children explore some of the dimensions of the problem in an appropriate way. In this first of three assemblies on the question 'Why do bad things happen?' we look at the role of choice. Choosing whether to do something helpful or harmful is a central issue in the classroom, so children should have no difficulty identifying with this.

RESOURCES

- a jigsaw-shaped piece of card with a drawing of a teddy bear on it. Photocopiable material is on page 247.
- a ball or a pencil.

A SAD STORY

Today's big question is a very big question. It is a very hard question. The question is, 'Why do bad things happen?' Sometimes people say, 'Why do bad things happen to good people? Doesn't God care?'

This is such a big question that it needs several jigsaw pieces to try to answer it. Even then, there will still be some holes left. Nobody really knows all the answers to this question, but that does not stop us thinking about it.

Here is the first jigsaw piece. It has a drawing of a teddy bear on it. That is to remind us of a story I am going to tell you. It is a true story.

A man was driving his car one day when he had an accident. The car skidded off the road and down an embankment. The man did not have his seatbelt on and he was killed. When the emergency services arrived, they found a teddy bear in the passenger seat. The bear was unharmed. Even though the man had not put his own seatbelt on, he had strapped the bear in with a belt.

The bad thing that happened in that story was a man getting killed. If he had put his seatbelt on he probably would have lived. That man chose not to do something he knew he should have done. He took more care of his teddy bear than he did of himself.

TALK ABOUT

1. Show the ball or pencil. It can be used to do good things, useful things, or bad things. Who can suggest some examples of good and bad things we can do with a ball/pencil?

2. Does anyone want to tell a story about when they did something silly with a ball/pencil — a story about themselves, not about someone else?

We can *choose* how we use this ball. The man in the story *chose* to belt his bear in and *chose* not to belt himself in. Some bad things happen because of what people choose to do or not do. We all need to think very seriously about the things we choose to do and not to do. Our choices can have very serious consequences. That's the first piece of the jigsaw.

WHY DO BAD THINGS HAPPEN? 2

BACKGROUND

In the last assembly we looked at choosing between good and bad. That choice can often be influenced by a third party. Much that is evil in the world occurs when people have pressure put on them to make the wrong choice. Children need to understand the concept of temptation and to think about how to reject it.

The concept of someone else attempting to influence our choices in the wrong direction is here introduced by thinking about the 'stranger danger' concept familiar to children.

RESOURCES

• a large jigsaw piece with a drawing of an apple on it. Photocopiable material is on page 248.

STRANGER DANGER

We are going to think some more today about the big question, 'Why do bad things happen?' and see if we can find another jigsaw-piece of the answer.

Do you remember the teddy bear in the car crash? The man in the car was killed because he chose not to put on his seatbelt. That was his own choice. But sometimes someone else tries to persuade us to choose to do the wrong thing.

Imagine you go out of the school gate this afternoon and a stranger offers you some sweets and a ride in his car. What would you say?

That stranger is trying to persuade you to do something you know you should not do. Can anyone think of other times when someone might try to persuade us to choose to do something wrong?

TEMPTATION

Show the jigsaw piece with the picture of the apple on it. This jigsaw piece will remind us of another story, a very well-known story. It is a story that comes right at the beginning of the Bible, in the book called Genesis.

In this story the first man, Adam, and the first woman, Eve, live in a beautiful garden in a place called Eden. The name Adam also means 'humans', both men and women. God gives Adam and Eve lots of good things which they can choose. He lets Adam choose the names of all the animals: the tame animals, the wild animals, and the birds. He gives Adam and Eve the choice of food: good fruit from lots of different trees. There is just one tree he warns them not to eat from. The fruit from this tree gives people knowledge of good and evil, and if they eat it they will eventually die.

Does anybody know what happens next in the story? (Pupils may be able to finish the story, with help from the teacher.)

One day a snake, the cleverest of all the animals, meets Eve and starts talking to her. He tells her that they won't die if they eat that fruit. 'God knows that if you eat the fruit from that tree, you will learn about good and evil. Then you will be like God!'

Eve is tempted by the snake's words. Both she and Adam eat some of the fruit. They start to think things they had not thought of before. They begin to feel awkward about having no clothes on, so they sew some leaves together to make themselves clothes. They feel guilty, and so they try to hide from God.

The end of the story is that Adam and Eve are forced out of the garden, where life was very pleasant and easy. They have to start working hard to grow food to eat. Life is much more difficult and sometimes painful. Eventually they both die.

Bad things happen in that story partly because of what the people choose to do. But there is also someone else in the story, the snake, who tempts them to choose the wrong thing. The snake is like the stranger telling you to do something you know you should not do. Sometimes really bad things happen when people listen to what others tell them instead of doing what they know inside is right.

TALK/THINK ABOUT

We all feel tempted to choose to do wrong things sometimes. It may be someone else tempting us, or just an idea that pops into our heads. What can we do to help us choose the right thing? (Just say no; move away from the temptation; tell a teacher or parent; pray to God for help.)

WHY DO BAD THINGS HAPPEN? 3

DOESN'T GOD CARE?

BACKGROUND

Our brief consideration of the question of suffering will inevitably seem inadequate. The jigsaw has more spaces than pieces! For Christians, perhaps the most important thing is not how close they come to answering the question, but that the life of Jesus shows that God knows and cares about suffering. They may not understand why he doesn't pull them out of the hole they are in, but they appreciate the fact that he jumps right in there beside them!

RESOURCES

o copies of the readings for a group to prepare
o a jigsaw piece with a drawing of a Cross on it. Photocopiable material is on pages 249 to 251.

GETTING READY

A group is needed to tell the rest of the class about some of the things that happened to Jesus.

INTRODUCTION

We have been asking the big question, Why do bad things happen? There are lots of reasons, but sometimes it is because we choose the wrong thing, or are tempted to make a wrong choice. When something bad does happen, we often ask the next big question, 'Doesn't God care?'

Doesn't God care when people fight and hurt each other? Doesn't God care when my dog got run over? Doesn't God care when people get treated unfairly? Is God so far away in heaven that he doesn't care what happens to us on earth?

Christians believe that God not only cares about us, he loves us so much that he sent Jesus into the world to show us he cares. Listen to some of the things that happened to Jesus.

THINGS THAT HAPPENED TO JESUS

Introduce the group to read the paragraphs they have prepared.

Names	Reading
. . . .	When Jesus was born, there was no room in the inn. Jesus' family knew what it was like to be homeless.
. . . .	King Herod sent soldiers to kill the babies in Bethlehem. Mary and Joseph had to take Jesus to another country to escape. They knew what it was like to be refugees.
. . . .	Jesus told people lots of things about God and about life, but a lot of important people would not listen. Jesus knew what it was like to tell the truth and not have people believe you.
. . . .	Jesus' cousin, John the Baptist, was killed in prison by another ruler called Herod. Jesus knew what it was like to have a tragic death in the family.
. . . .	Judas betrayed Jesus, and his other friends ran away when the soldiers came to arrest him. Jesus knew what it was like to have friends let you down.
. . . .	After Jesus was arrested, people told lies about him and did not give him a fair trial. He knew what it was like to be treated unfairly.
. . . .	The soldiers blindfolded Jesus and beat him up and made fun of him. Jesus knew what it was like to be bullied.
. . . .	Jesus was hung on a cross and left to die. He knew what it was like to suffer terrible pain.

JIGSAW

Show the jigsaw piece with the Cross on it. Christians believe that the Cross tells us that because God cares, he sent Jesus to share in the bad things we go through. When it hurts, Jesus knows what it is like. That is why there are lots of people in the world who say that Jesus is their best friend. They know that whatever happens, Jesus knows what it feels like and they can talk to him about it.

177

TALK/THINK ABOUT

1. Think of some times when you were hurt or upset. Has a friend ever been able to help you because the same thing had happened to them and they knew what it was like?

2. Do you think God wants all of us to care for each other? How can we do that?

IF I DO SOMETHING SILLY, CAN GOD PUT IT RIGHT?

BACKGROUND

Feelings of guilt can be crippling. Children can feel false guilt, as in instances where they feel in some way responsible for parents separating, or genuinely guilty of some hurtful action. Christian understanding is that although actions can have serious and long-lasting consequences, there is nothing that cannot be redeemed. The key seems to be a partnership, with a genuine turning away from wrong on the human side, and the power of infinite love to bring good even from evil on God's side. Persian rug-makers provide us with a satisfying illustration of that partnership.

RESOURCES

- a large sheet of paper divided into four and fixed to a board
- felt or marker pens for four people
- a homemade rug as an example, if possible
- a blank jigsaw piece and marker pen. Photocopiable material is on page 238.

SYMMETRICAL PATTERNS

When we looked at why bad things happen, we said that one of the reasons was that people choose to do things they know are wrong. Perhaps lots of us thought of times when we made bad choices. So today's big question is, 'If I do something silly, can God put it right?'

To help us think about this, we are going to start with something a bit tricky, something where people are bound to make mistakes.

Provide three volunteers with felt or marker pens and allocate each one a quarter of a large sheet of paper fixed to a board. Remind the children of butterfly paintings or other work they have done on symmetry.

Slowly draw lines and shapes in one quarter of the paper. The volunteers must try to match the drawings in their corners to make a symmetrical, mirror-image pattern. Either work continuously or do one shape at a time depending on the ability of the pupils to follow.

Comment on the difficulty of doing this accurately.

WORKING WITH FATHER

There is one part of the world where whole families work together doing something like this, only instead of drawing, they work pieces of wool into a backing to make rugs. This country used to be called Persia, and handmade Persian rugs are world-famous. They can be very expensive, and people sometimes hang them on a wall rather than put them on the floor. They are too good to walk on!

This is how they are made. The father works on one end of the rug, and the children work on the other end. He tells them what they have to do to make the pattern he has in his mind. But because they are still learning, they make mistakes. This is how the family earns a living, so the father could get angry and punish them. But he doesn't. Instead, the father watches the children's work. When he sees a mistake, he does the same thing at his end of the rug and

180

turns it into a new pattern. When the rug is finished, it has a perfect pattern. No-one could ever tell that the children had made any mistakes!

This seems to be a bit like how Christians understand God works with people, his children. He knows that they are going to make mistakes, do silly things. (Show jigsaw piece and draw a cross on it.) The mistakes can't be rubbed out, but God can take them and make a new pattern, like the father rugmaker. And in the end, God's pattern will be perfect. (Put a tick next to the cross on the jigsaw piece.)

There is one thing we can do to help sort out the pattern quickly: when we realise we have made a mistake, we can admit it and say sorry. That makes everybody feel better, and it stops the mistake getting worse.

TALK/THINK ABOUT

1. Do you think the children who make the rugs don't care if they make mistakes, or do you think they try to be as good as their father?

2. Do you think when we do something silly we should say, 'I don't care!' or should we try to make as few mistakes as possible?

WHY DID MY HAMSTER DIE?

BACKGROUND

The day after the Hillsborough football stadium disaster, in which so many Liverpool fans died, one of the authors was due to speak to a large meeting of Boys Brigade groups in Nottingham. Some of the boys had been at the match, many of the others were Nottingham Forest supporters. The issue of death had to be faced. From time to time, that is true in any family or school. At such moments, it is helpful if the taboo on talking about death has already been broken, if the issue has begun to be talked and thought about. The death of a pet allows children to begin to experience the feelings and explore the issues associated with death.

RESOURCES

+ a fish-finger packet (empty)
+ a jigsaw piece with a drawing or a cut-out picture of a pet. Photocopiable material is on page 252.

TALK ABOUT

Who has had a pet that died? How did you feel when your pet died? Did you bury it in the garden?

Give the children time to talk around these questions.

FIVE SPARROWS FOR TWO PENNIES

When a pet we have loved dies, we may ask questions like, 'Why did God let my hamster die?' or, 'Doesn't God care my cat got run over?' or, 'Do animals go to heaven?' These are big questions for us. (Show the jigsaw piece with a picture of a pet.)

In the time of Jesus, many people had a few animals in the house. They might have had one or two sheep or goats, or a few chickens, or a donkey. These were more like farm animals than pets, but there were dogs as well. Jesus never spoke about pets, but he did say something one day about sparrows. It sounds strange to us. Listen.

'When five sparrows are sold, they only cost two pennies. But God does not forget any of them' (Luke 12:6).

Has anyone got any idea what the sparrows were being sold for? . . . To eat! There can't be much meat on a sparrow. It must be like a very tiny chicken.

If Jesus was talking to us today, he wouldn't tell us about sparrows. We don't eat sparrows! I wonder what he would say? Perhaps it would be (show fish-finger packet): 'You can buy ten fish-fingers in the supermarket for only 75p. But God doesn't forget even one of the fish that were caught to make them.'

God doesn't forget a tiny sparrow sold in an eastern market. He doesn't forget even one of the millions of fish caught in the sea. Do you think he forgets your hamster that you loved very much? Or your budgerigar that you taught to talk?

The Bible does not tell us what happens when animals die. It does not tell us if there are animals in heaven. But it does tell us how God provides food for them and looks after them. And it does tell us that God does not forget them.

A PRAYER

A child might read this prayer. Others can agree by saying 'amen', if they want to.

> **Father God, Thank you that you made animals for us**
> **to love and care for.**
> **Thank you for the fun and friendship we get from our pets.**
> **Comfort us when we feel sad because one of them dies.**
> **Thank you that you don't forget even one of our pets.** Amen.

NOTE

Jesus goes on to say, 'Yes, God even knows how many hairs you have on your head. Don't be afraid. You are worth much more than many sparrows.' In the event of needing to talk with the children about a death in the school or of someone close to a child, this could be helpful. If God does not forget a sparrow, or one of our pets, how much more does he care for a person we know and love.

MATERIAL FOR PHOTOCOPYING

The following pages reproduce the sections of the assemblies for pupils to prepare and the associated charts, pictures and craft instructions. They are designed for ease of photocopying.

Setting the photocopier enlargement feature to 130% will bring these pages up to A4 size if required.

This book has been specially bound to sustain repeated photocopying.

LEARNING TO WAIT 1

TWO IMPATIENT BROTHERS

GETTING READY TO HELP WITH ASSEMBLY

You are going to help with the assembly by acting the parts of twin brothers in a play. The quieter brother, JACOB, is making some vegetable soup. Can you find a saucepan or a bowl? The rougher, tougher brother is ESAU. He arrives back from a hunting trip starving.

PLAY: THE BIG SOUP DEAL

JACOB   (*He is stirring the soup, tasting it, adding some salt.*)

ESAU   (*Comes in noisily, moaning.*) I didn't catch a thing. Not even a rabbit. And I'm starving. Mmm. That smells good. Hey, Jacob, give me a bowl.

JACOB   Make your own. There's not enough here for you.

ESAU   Oh go on. If I'd caught a rabbit or a partridge, I'd have shared it with you. I've been out since sunrise. I'm weak with hunger.

JACOB   Okay, I'll make a deal with you. I'll sell you some soup.

ESAU   Anything. Just give me some soup.

JACOB   You're the oldest. You'll be head of the family when Dad dies. Sell me the right of the oldest son so that I'll be head of the family.

ESAU   Look, I'm almost dead from hunger. Being the head of the family and all Dad's money won't help me if I die.

JACOB   Right, promise me then.

ESAU   I promise.

JACOB   You promise I can be head of the family and have your share of Dad's money?

ESAU   (*Shouting.*) Yes, I promise. Just give me some soup!

STRENGTH AND WEAKNESS 1

A NERVOUS LEADER

GETTING READY TO HELP WITH ASSEMBLY

You are going to act out a TV interview. Decide who is going to be the interviewer and Gideon.

Gideon is very nervous at first. You can show this by fidgeting, biting your nails, stroking your hair. Get more confident later in the interview.

Check anything you do not understand with your teacher.

Set up the scene with two chairs, a table, and a pretend microphone. You will also need a woolly jumper. Rehearse the interview.

PLAY: GIDEON'S EXPERIMENT

A TV interview

INTERVIEWER Welcome to Newsworld. The latest news from the war zone is that the Midianites are continuing their invasion and stealing all the food they can find. Many people have run away, too frightened to fight.

But there are some promising signs. As we reported yesterday, a young man called Gideon has issued a call to people to join him in resisting the invaders. He also seems to be something of a scientist. We have invited him into the studio this evening. Mr. Gideon, welcome to Newsworld.

GIDEON *(Comes in and sits down very nervously)* Er, thank you. Good, um, evening.

188

INTERVIEWER	Well, Mr. Gideon, I understand this all started in a winepress. That sounds rather strange. Were you making wine?
GIDEON	Er, no.
INTERVIEWER	Well, some new jam using grapes perhaps?
GIDEON	Er, not exactly.
INTERVIEWER	Well, what were you doing in that winepress?
GIDEON	Threshing wheat, sir.
INTERVIEWER	Wheat? To make flour? In a winepress?
GIDEON	Er, yes, yes . . .
INTERVIEWER	Is this some new scientific invention?
GIDEON	Er, no, not really. You see, I was scared.
INTERVIEWER	So you were hiding in a winepress?
GIDEON	Yes, so they wouldn't get me. Those Midianites. They're such bullies. No one can stand up to them.
INTERVIEWER	Yes, quite, I understand. You were hiding in the winepress so your wheat would not get stolen. Let's move on quickly to the experiment with the woolly jumper. Do you have it with you? (*Gideon shows the woolly jumper.*)
	Thank you. Perhaps you can explain to the viewers what you did with this jumper.
GIDEON	(*More confidently.*) Well it all started when God told me . . .
INTERVIEWER	(*Interrupting.*) Excuse me, you said **God** — was he in this experiment?
GIDEON	Oh very much so, sir (*growing in confidence*). God told me to lead the Israelites against the Midianites.
INTERVIEWER	But I thought you were, um, scared of the enemy?
GIDEON	I am. I mean, I was. Well, that was before . . . now I know that God is with me.
INTERVIEWER	How do you know?
GIDEON	Well, I thought God was telling me to lead the Israelites, and I was frightened. But the idea wouldn't go away, so I decided on an experiment.

189

(Picks up jumper and demonstrates.)

You see, I said to God, 'I'll leave this on the ground overnight. In the morning, if the ground is dry and the woolly jumper is wet with dew, then I will know that I must lead Israel.'

INTERVIEWER And was the jumper wet?

GIDEON Yes.

INTERVIEWER And the ground was dry?

GIDEON Yes.

INTERVIEWER So, what did you decide then?

GIDEON To do it again.

INTERVIEWER That sounds like good scientific practice!

GIDEON Yes, but I changed it a bit. I said to God, 'This time, make the jumper dry and the ground wet.'

INTERVIEWER And what happened this second time?

GIDEON The jumper was dry and the ground was wet.

INTERVIEWER Very interesting, Mr. Gideon. As a result of those experiments what are you going to do?

GIDEON I'm going to lead the Israelites against the Midianites, with God's help. In fact, I want everyone who is listening and prepared to stand up against these bullies to meet me tomorrow.

INTERVIEWER Thank you. *(Turning to face the audience.)* So could this be a turning point in the struggle against the Midianites? Can young Gideon really free us from this menace? We'll keep you informed of all the latest news here on Newsworld. Good night.

STRENGTH AND WEAKNESS 2

GIDEON LEARNS TO SUBTRACT AND DIVIDE

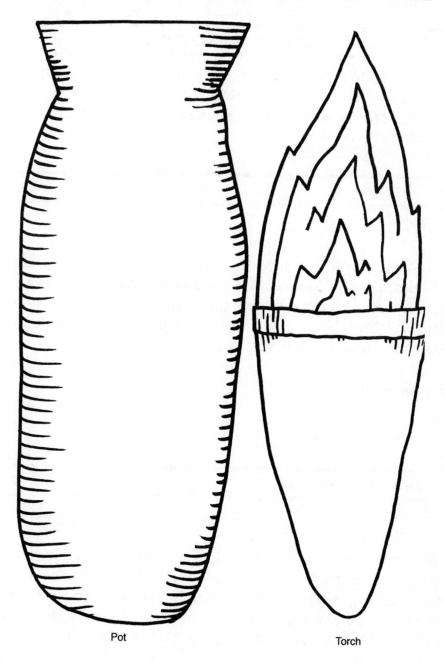

Pot

Torch

HELPING SOMEONE IN NEED

THE STORY OF RUTH

GETTING READY TO HELP WITH ASSEMBLY

You are going to read some imaginary letters to a problem page in a newspaper. There are three letters to read: from RUTH, from THE EDITOR, and from BOAZ. (Boaz rhymes with 'go as'.) Practise reading clearly and slowly.

FIRST LETTER

Dear Sir,

I am a young woman from Moab, living with my mother-in-law in Israel. Her name is Naomi. My husband has died, but I won't go back to my own country as my mother-in-law would have no-one to look after her. Now we are very poor and worried because we have nothing to eat. What shall we do?

Yours sincerely,

Ruth.

ANSWER IN THE NEWSPAPER

Dear Ruth,

I am sorry to hear of the difficulties you are having since your husband died. But it is good to read your letter and discover your kindness to your mother-in-law, Naomi. Not many young women are as faithful as you are these days. I am sure God will bless you because of your kindness and show you the way forward. Listen to your mother-in-law's advice, because she is older and wiser than you, and God will speak through her. Please let us know how you get on.

Yours sincerely,

The Editor.

THIRD LETTER

Dear Sir,

Some time ago, a young woman called Ruth wrote to you with a problem. I want you to know that your advice to her was very good. All her problems are solved, because she is now my dear and beautiful wife! Let me explain what happened.

Naomi is my cousin. She returned to our village of Bethlehem after living in another country for several years. It was a sad time, because her husband had died and then her son, Ruth's first husband, also died. She felt very bitter. If it had not been for Ruth, I don't know what she would have done.

I first saw Ruth when she was collecting fallen grains of barley in my field. It was all she and Naomi had to live on. I told my workers to leave some corn for her so they would have enough to eat. As the days of the harvest passed, I grew to admire Ruth and then to love her. Finally, I asked her to marry me.

It was only later that I learned that my cousin Naomi had been scheming to bring us together. It was Naomi who advised Ruth to collect the barley in my field and make sure that I noticed her. I am very glad she did! You were quite right to tell Ruth to listen to her mother-in-law's advice.

Yours gratefully,

Boaz.

HEARING AND DOING 2
THE BOYS WHO WOULD NOT LISTEN

GETTING READY TO HELP WITH ASSEMBLY

You are going to help with the next class assembly. You have three things to do:

1. Make a Time-Traveller's helmet.

2. Practice reading a report by a Time-Traveller.

3. Four of you make up a short play.

JOB 1

Make a Time-Traveller's helmet. You could use a small box as the base. Make sure it fits on your head without

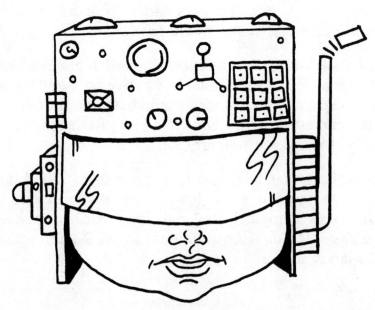

A Time-Traveller's helmet

falling down over your eyes. Cover it with coloured or shiny paper. Stick things on it from the scrap-box to represent an aerial or bits of strange electronic equipment.

JOB 2: TIME-TRAVELLER'S REPORT

The Time-Traveller. You are going to read this report. Think of a suitable voice for a Time-Traveller. Practice reading clearly.

☒ The date is 1,000 years before Jesus was born.

☒ Place: some hills in Israel. It is hot. The grass is brown.

☒ I can see some big, square tents. Some women in the tents are making bread. The bread looks like fat pancakes.

☒ I can see some children. They don't go to school. They are in the hills. They are looking after little flocks of sheep and goats. I think they do that all day long.

☒ Now I can see a family. They are walking along a dusty track. They are taking a sheep with them. It looks like the fattest sheep in the flock.

☒ The family arrives at the Temple at Shiloh. They have come to say thank you to God for looking after them. They also want to say sorry for the wrong things they have done. They give the sheep to the priest for a sacrifice. It's like giving something back to God.

☒ The priest has to be a butcher. He cuts up the meat and burns some of the best meat on a fire on the altar. Then he puts the rest in a big pot to boil as a stew.

☒ When the meat is cooked, the priest comes with a big fork. He sticks it in the pot and spears a big piece of meat. That is the share for him and his children.

☒ The family sits down and eats the rest of the stew. It's like a party. They all feel happy because they have said thank you to God and sorry to God. The sacrifice shows they really mean it.

☒ End of report. Returning to the present.

You are going to make up a play about what happens when a family comes to the Temple at Shiloh and Eli's two sons do not treat them right. The characters in the play are HOPHNI and PHINEAS (say: 'hoff-nee' and 'fin-ee-us'), their father ELI, and one or two VISITORS to the Temple. (If you want, you can read the story in the Bible in the First book of Samuel, chapter 2, verses 12 to 17 and 22 to 25.)

You will need a large bowl or saucepan and a very large fork. Borrow them from the kitchen or make the fork and use a box for the saucepan.

Play: Lucky dip

SCENE 1:

A VISITOR (or a family) comes to the Temple to offer a sacrifice. HOPHNI and PHINEAS say they want their portion. The visitor says they can take their lucky-dip from the pot with the big fork as normal. HOPHNI and PHINEAS say they want the best steak or the best joint for roasting, not just any old piece of boiled meat. They threaten to beat the visitor up if they don't get what they want.

SCENE 2:

The visitor goes to ELI, the priest. He is upset because he has come to pray to God and offer a sacrifice, but he is being bullied. Hophni and Phineas are breaking God's laws. ELI is shocked and says he will speak to his sons.

SCENE 3:

ELI tells HOPHNI and PHINEAS off. They are hurting other people and that makes God unhappy, too. Who will protect them if they break God's laws like this? When ELI leaves, the two boys laugh at the old man behind his back. They are not going to listen to him. They decide to go on demanding the best pieces of meat.

HEARING AND DOING 3

SAMUEL HEARS AND OBEYS

HELPING WITH THE ASSEMBLY

The teacher is going to read a story about the boy Samuel when he lived at the Temple. Half-way through the story, you read the parts of SAMUEL and ELI the priest. You could act these parts out as you read them. Arrange two tables to lie on as beds, or lie on the floor.

TEACHER One night he woke up to hear his name being called. 'Samuel!'

SAMUEL (*Sitting up*) Here I am. (*Getting up and going to Eli*) Here I am. You called me.

ELI I didn't call you. Go back and lie down again. (*Samuel lies down again*)

TEACHER Samuel supposed he must have been dreaming. He was just dropping off to sleep when he heard his name being called again, 'Samuel!'

SAMUEL (*Getting up and going to Eli*) Here I am. You called me.

ELI I didn't call you. Go back and lie down again.

TEACHER Then it happened a third time. By now Eli was wide awake. He realised that it must be God calling the boy. 'Samuel!'

SAMUEL (*Getting up and going to Eli*) Here I am. You called me.

ELI Go back and lie down again. And if he calls you again say, 'Speak, Lord, for your servant is listening.' (*Samuel lies down again*)

TEACHER I wonder how Samuel felt as he went back to lie down on his mat this time? He didn't have long to wait. 'Samuel! Samuel!' said the voice.

SAMUEL Speak, for your servant is listening.

TEACHER Then God began to speak to Samuel. It was a hard message.

HEARING AND DOING 4

ARE YOU LISTENING?

You are going to make up a play for the next class
assembly and record it like a radio play. You will need a tape-
recorder with a microphone and a tape. Choose one person to
operate the tape-recorder. When you are ready, find a quiet place
to record the play. Record everyone speaking first and then listen
to check if the recording is loud enough.

Make up a play about the Green Cross Code and someone who did
not listen properly.

SCENE 1:

You could start with one person being the Police School Liaison
Officer coming into school to remind pupils about the Green Cross
Code. Someone else could be the teacher reminding everybody to
remember what they heard when they go home.

SCENE 2:

It is home time, with people shouting goodbye to each other. There
could be an ice-cream van outside school — can somebody play
ice-cream van music on a xylophone or recorder?

SCENE 3:

Two children could be talking about buying an ice-cream. One
says to remember the Green Cross Code but the other is in too
much of a hurry. There is an accident. Can you make noises like
a car skidding and an ambulance coming?

SCENE 4:

You could have a scene at the hospital, or a reporter asking people what happened, or the head teacher talking in assembly the next day.

Could you make up a jingle to finish with to remind people to use the Green Cross Code?

David and Goliath

LIVING IN FAMILIES 2

A GOOD FRIEND

David's friend Jonathan

LIVING IN FAMILIES 3

HELP FROM THE FAMILY

David's wife Michal

LIVING IN FAMILIES 3

HELP FROM THE FAMILY

David's wife Abigail

LIVING IN FAMILIES 4

Uriah is killed in battle

SOLVING PROBLEMS 1

THE KING'S PROBLEM

You are going to illustrate the first part of the story of
The beauty queen and the three problems. These are the things you
will need to find or make:

- two crowns, a larger one for the king and a smaller one for the
  queen.
- pictures of five or six beautiful girls. Cut them out and stick
  them on paper or card.
- pictures of fine clothes and jewellery. Cut them out and stick
  them on large pieces of paper.

One or two people will also need to practise walking
with a book on their heads, and miming putting on
make-up.

Look at the story to see how all these things fit in. You have to
show them at the right time, when the teacher tells you.

The teacher reads	Your actions
What do you think King Xerxes did? Well, he decided to hold a kind of beauty contest.	*None.*
He sent throughout his empire for the most beautiful girls to come to his palace so that he might choose one of them as the new queen.	*Show pictures of beautiful girls.*
Each one was trained to walk properly.	*Walk with book on head.*

Each one was taught to put on make-up and given sweet-smelling perfume.

Mime putting on make-up.

Each one could choose the clothes to wear and jewellery to make herself even more beautiful.

Show pictures of clothes and jewellery.

Mmm. It was difficult. 'Which one?' thought King Xerxes. 'Which one shall I choose to be my new queen?' They were all so lovely. But Xerxes needed someone who would not let him down as Queen Vashti had done; a new queen who would not oppose him. He pondered, he spent time with each girl. Finally he chose a girl called Esther.

Show pictures of girls again.

Esther was a Jew. Her people had been brought to Persia as captives a few years before. But Esther did not tell the king she was Jewish. She kept it a secret.

None.

King Xerxes placed the crown on his new queen's head.

King places crown on girl's head.

It was time for another party, Esther's party. He even declared a holiday for his whole kingdom. He wanted everyone to know he had solved his problem.

206

SOLVING PROBLEMS 3

ESTHER'S SOLUTION

GETTING READY TO HELP WITH ASSEMBLY

You are going to prepare a play called *Esther's solution* for the next class assembly.

JOB 1

Make or find some props for the play. These are the things you will need:

- the two crowns for the king and queen. See if you can find clothes for them in the dressing-up box.
- a sceptre for the king. Cover a ruler with gold or yellow paper.
- a banquet. Cut out pictures of food from magazines and stick them on a large piece of card or paper.

JOB 2

Rehearse the play. The characters in the play are: the KING, QUEEN ESTHER, HAMAN, and one or two SERVANTS.

Play: Esther's solution

(King Xerxes is sitting on his throne with his sceptre in his hand. Haman is nearby. Queen Esther enters and waits for the king to see her. She is nervous.)

KING My lady Esther, approach the royal throne. (*Holds out the sceptre. Esther comes, touches the end of it, and bows.*) What is it, Queen Esther? What do you want of me?

ESTHER If it pleases you, my king, I would like to invite you and your chief minister Haman to a banquet.

KING It does please me. Come quickly, Haman, so we can do

what Esther asks. (*Haman bows as the king and queen walk out.*)

HAMAN The queen noticed me. She did not invite any of the other ministers. I'm the most important. I must go and tell my wife. (*Haman leaves. One or two servants bring on the food. The king and queen follow, then Haman.*)

KING What a wonderful feast you have prepared for us, Esther. Tell me, what do you want? I will give you as much as half my kingdom.

ESTHER My king, I hope you are pleased with me. If you are, this is what I ask. Let me live, and let my people live, too. I and all my people are going to be killed.

KING What! Who dares do such a thing? Where is he?

ESTHER Our enemy is this wicked Haman! (*Esther points to Haman, who falls on his knees, terrified. The king is very angry.*)

KING Haman! How dare you threaten the queen! I am too angry to think. I am going into the garden to decide what to do. (*The king leaves. Haman crawls to Esther and grabs her around the knees, begging for his life.*)

HAMAN Queen Esther, please spare me! Save me! Please! (*The king comes back in. He thinks Haman is attacking Esther.*)

KING You villain! Would you even attack the queen in my own palace? Guards! Take this man away. (*The servants come and take Haman away.*)

KING My lady, it is Haman who will be killed, not you. All your family and your people will be safe. I am going to give you everything Haman owned. And Mordecai will be one of my chief ministers. Come. (*The king and queen leave.*)

SOLVING PROBLEMS 4

THE LOST T-SHIRT

HELPING WITH ASSEMBLY

Six people read these parts: TEACHER, NARRATOR, CHILD 1, CHILD 2, CHILD 3, CHILD 4. The play is in two parts. Be ready to read when the teacher tells you.

Part One

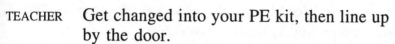

TEACHER Get changed into your PE kit, then line up by the door.

NARRATOR Mrs Brooks glanced quickly round the room to check that everyone had heard, smiling as she saw Michelle struggle to undo a knot in her trainers.

CHILD 1 Mrs Brooks, I can't do PE, I've hurt my foot.

CHILD 2 Mrs Brooks, can I go to the toilet?

CHILD 3 Mrs Brooks, my sister borrowed my trainers. Can I go to her class to ask for them?

NARRATOR Mrs Brooks smiled or nodded in response to each question as she helped Michelle untie the knot.

CHILD 4 Mrs Brooks, I've lost my T-shirt.

NARRATOR Donna stood in front of her teacher looking tearful. What should she do now?

Wait as your teacher explains things. Be ready to read when you are told.

Part Two

TEACHER	Does your T-shirt have your name on it, Donna?
CHILD 4	No. But I'd know it if I saw it. It's got a tear in the collar and a red felt-tip pen mark on the back.
TEACHER	Yes, well, having your name on would help. Have you looked in the cloakroom?
CHILD 4	Yes, Miss.
TEACHER	Under the cupboards?
CHILD 4	Yes.
TEACHER	Have you asked your friends if they have seen it?
CHILD 4	Yes.
TEACHER	(*Claps hands*). Quiet a moment, please. Donna has lost her T-shirt. Would you all look in your bags to see if you have picked it up by mistake.
CHILD 2	Donna's friend Charlotte might have it. She borrowed it last week.
TEACHER	Thank you. Now Donna, go and ask Charlotte if she still has it.
NARRATOR	Donna goes out and returns holding a T-shirt and smiling.

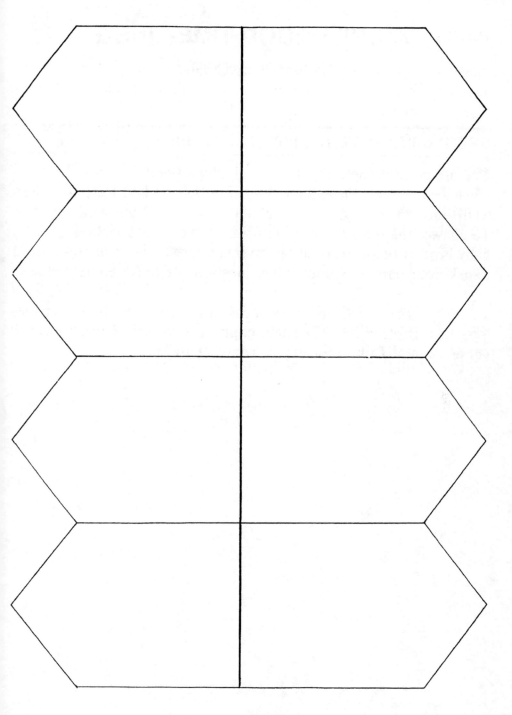

Time-Line labels

A CHILDHOOD TIME-LINE 2

A BABY IS BORN

GETTING READY TO HELP WITH ASSEMBLY

You are going to help the class think about the differences between when Jesus was born and a baby being born today. Here is a chart to fill in with some questions about Jesus and about a baby today. To answer the questions about a baby today you can think about a baby brother or sister, or about an imaginary baby. You might need to ask your parents some of the questions or make some guesses.

To answer the questions about Jesus in the chart on the next page, look in a Bible. Find **Matthew chapter 1 verse 18 to chapter 2 verse 12**, and **Luke chapter 2, verses 1 to 20.**

QUESTIONS	JESUS	A CHILD TODAY
1. Who told Mum about the baby?		
2. Where was the baby born?		
3. What transport was used to get Mum there?		
4. When was this?		
5. What clothes did the baby have?		
6. Where was the baby put to sleep?		
7. Who else was there?		
8. What visitors came?		
9. What presents did they bring?		

A CHILDHOOD TIME-LINE 4

LEARNING WITH ADULTS

HELPING WITH ASSEMBLY

One of the things Jesus would have learned at school and at home was the Ten Commandments. The Ten Commandments are God's rules to help us live good lives. Practise reading them ready for assembly.

Reader 1 I am the Lord your God. You must not have any other gods except me.
You must not make for yourselves any idols.
You must not use the name of the Lord your God thoughtlessly.

Reader 2 You may work and get everything done during six days each week. But the seventh day is a day of rest to honour the Lord your God.
Honour your father and your mother.
You must not murder anyone.

Reader 3 Be faithful to the one you marry.
You must not steal.
You must not tell lies about your neighbour in court.
You must not want to take anything that belongs to your neighbour.

Jesus at a wedding in Cana

SPECIAL DAYS 2

JESUS HELPS A DISABLED PERSON

GETTING READY TO HELP WITH ASSEMBLY

For the story in the next class assembly we need a model of a house like Jesus lived in. Your job is to make the model house and some cut-out people. Decide who is going to make the stairs and who is going to make the people.

Job 1

Find a cardboard box. Cut out a door and windows or paint them. Look at the picture to help you. If it is thick cardboard, ask a teacher or helper to cut it.

Cut a hole in the flat roof of the house, then tape it back again so that it will come out easily. Make the hole big enough for the man on the mat to go through.

Job 2

Cut a strip of thin card twice as long as the side of the box. Bend it to make a staircase like in the picture. Tape it to the side of the house.

Job 3

Draw some people on thin card and cut them out. Make them like the ones in the picture. Colour them in.

Cut two pieces of wool twice as long as the height of the box. Practise wrapping the wool round the cut-out man on the mat and pretending to lower him through a hole in the roof without dropping him.

SPECIAL DAYS 2

JESUS HELPS A DISABLED PERSON

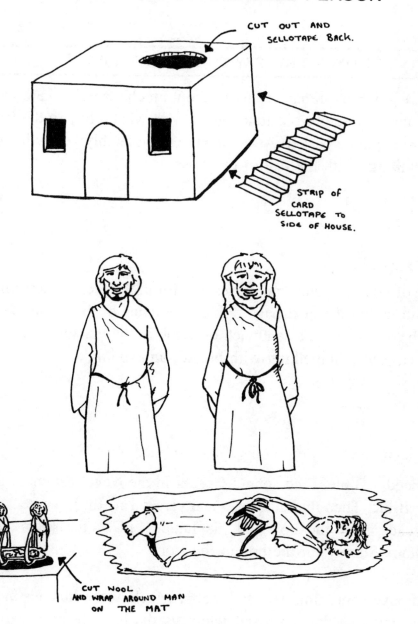

A model to make

SPECIAL DAYS 3

JESUS FEEDS A BIG CROWD

GETTING READY TO HELP WITH THE ASSEMBLY

You are going to prepare a survey about lunchboxes. You are going to compare three of your lunchboxes with what a boy in the Bible had in his picnic basket. At the next class assembly you will share your findings with the rest of the class.

Job 1

Three of you get your lunchboxes and fill in the Picnic and Lunchbox Survey on the next page. Fill in the name of the owner of the lunchbox. If there is a sandwich or a cob in the lunchbox, tick the box that says, 'Something with bread', and so on.

Job 2

You need a Bible. Find John's Gospel in the New Testament part of the Bible. Then find chapter 6 and verses 1 to 13. In verse 9 you will read about the boy and his lunch. Fill in the Picnic and Lunchbox Survey for the boy in the story.

If you have some time left, talk about which of the lunches in the survey you like the most and which is the best 'healthy eating' lunch.

Picnic and Lunchbox Survey

Owner	Something with bread	Fruit or vegetable	Fish, egg or meat	Food in packets	Other things
1					
2					
3					
The boy in John chapter 6 verse 9					

SPECIAL DAYS 4

THE WEATHERMAN'S NIGHTMARE

GETTING READY TO HELP WITH ASSEMBLY

You are going to do a play for the next class assembly called *The Weatherman's Nightmare*. Two good readers can prepare the play, and other people can make the weather map and symbols.

Job 1

On a big piece of paper, make a copy of the weather map showing Lake Galilee. Make the outline good and strong so that all the class can see it. Draw, colour, and cut out some weather symbols from stiff paper or thin card. You need two sun symbols, two black storm-cloud symbols, and a wind arrow.

Before the assembly, fix the map to a wall or board with Blu-tack and put Blu-tack on the back of the symbols ready for the weatherman.

Job 2

Two readers prepare this play. The weatherman stands in front of the map (when it is ready). Have the symbols ready to stick on. The Producer could do the telephone sound effects, or someone else in the group.

Play: The Weatherman's Nightmare

WEATHERMAN Good evening. Here is the local weather forecast for the Galilee area. Well, all is calm over northern Israel tonight, blue skies and plenty of evening sunshine. (*Put on sun shapes.*)

That means it will be good for sailing and fishing on the lake tonight.

(*Sound effect: phone ringing.*) Oh! Excuse me . . . yes, speaking . . . are you sure? You are? . . . Alright . . . (*Replace phone.*)

I am very sorry, but there has been a sudden change in the weather. Lake Galilee has been hit by a tremendous storm, with very strong winds sweeping in from the north-east and bringing heavy rain. (*Put on cloud shapes and arrows.*) Fisherman are advised NOT to take their boats out as conditions are getting worse. The storm can be expected to reach hurricane strength in . . .

(*Sound effect: phone ringing.*) . . . Oh! please excuse me this is most unusual . . . what? . . . but that can't be right . . . you told me to give a hurricane warning . . . who? He did what? . . . Who is this Jesus? (*Replace phone.*)

. . . er, where was I? . . . oh yes there's been a slight misunderstanding. (*Take off clouds.*) It seems that the storm has disappeared. I can't explain it . . . it just can't happen like that . . . it's incredible . . . I can't cope with this. I'm going to leave it to the Producer to sort out.

PRODUCER Here is a news flash. A violent storm hit Lake Galillee this evening without warning. Fishermen in a boat on the lake feared they were going to drown. They said they had never been out in a storm like it. The well-known teacher, Jesus of Nazareth, was also in the boat. One of the fishermen described how Jesus just told the storm to be quiet and it died down straight away. Others in the boat confessed that they were really shaken. They said they had never seen anything like it in their lives. That is the end of the news flash.

SPECIAL DAYS 4

THE WEATHERMAN'S NIGHTMARE

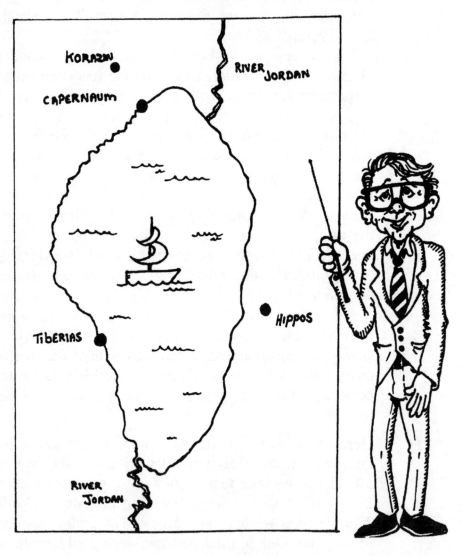

STORIES TO MAKE YOU THINK 2

A FARMER COMPLAINS

HELPING WITH ASSEMBLY

Here are two letters for you to read. Get ready to read them when the teacher asks you.

Reader 1

Korazin,
Galilee

Dear Sir,

I am writing to complain about this year's harvest. My family and I have been working from early morning to late at night, and still we've not had a good harvest. I think it must be your seed. It's just not good enough.

What can a poor farmer do if the seed does not produce good wheat? My family will go hungry this winter with the little harvest which has grown.

Sadly yours,

Reuben, a poor farmer.

Reader 2

Tiberias,
Galilee

Dear farmer Reuben,

I am very sorry that you did not have a good harvest this year. I hope that your family will have enough to eat.

Can I ask you a few questions? Did you look where your seed landed when you were sowing it? Did some land on the path so the birds could see it and swoop down to eat it? Did some seeds land on rocky ground with not much soil so that it soon dried up in the hot sun? Did some of it land in patches of thorns so that it got choked by the weeds?

It is not always the fault of the seed, sometimes there are other things to think about. I am trusting that enough seed did fall on good ground to produce wheat to feed your family in the coming months.

Hopefully yours,

Grobag and Haystack, Seed Merchants

MONEY! MONEY! MONEY! 3

SHARE WITH ME!

GETTING READY TO HELP WITH THE ASSEMBLY

You are going to help with an assembly about sharing. Three or four people will give a simple demonstration in sharing, while the rest of the class guess what you are doing. One person will read a story Jesus told.

Job 1

Collect some of your own belongings. These can be coats, gloves and scarves if it is that time of year, or felt-tips, rubbers and rulers. Also get some plastic money, if possible.

One person has all the things you have collected. The other two or three stand in a line with their hands out. The first person shares the belongings and the money out among the others. You can say things like, 'One coat for you, and one for you. Ten pence for you, and ten pence for you.' Don't say the word *sharing*. The rest of the class have to guess this.

Job 2

Practise reading this story. Read it slowly and clearly. You might imagine you are an actor reading it and put in lots of expression.

There was a rich man who had some land, which grew a good crop of food. The rich man thought to himself, 'What will I do? I have no place to keep all my crops.' Then he said, 'I know what I will do. I will tear down my barns and build bigger ones! I will put all my grain and other goods together in my new barns. Then I can say to myself, I have enough things stored to last for many years. Rest, eat, drink, and enjoy life!'

But God said to that man, 'Foolish man! Tonight you will die. So who will get those things you have prepared for yourself?'

That story is found in the book of Luke, chapter 12, verses 16 to 20.

MONEY! MONEY! MONEY! 4

JESUS AT THE TEMPLE

GETTING READY TO HELP WITH THE ASSEMBLY

You are going to be a Time-Traveller and read this Time-Traveller's report.

You will need a Time-Traveller's helmet. (See page 194) Practise reading this report ready for the class assembly.

- ☒ The year is 30 CE. The month is April.
- ☒ I am in a big crowd of people moving up some steps to an enormous wall. The wall is as high as a twelve-storey block of flats.
- ☒ We go through a great archway in the wall and up lots more steps. The people in the crowd look tired, but excited. Some have come a long way to be here for the festival.
- ☒ At last we come out into the sunshine. We are on top of a platform so big it could hold nearly thirty football pitches.
- ☒ Close to the centre of the platform is the Temple King Herod built. It is covered in gold, and so dazzling in the sunlight that I can hardly look at it. Some of the children who have just come up the steps are open-mouthed in astonishment.
- ☒ Near me is a family who have come from a village in Galilee. They have come to the Temple to offer a sacrifice to God to show how sorry they are for the wrong things they have done.
- ☒ The father is going to buy two pigeons. That is the cheapest sacrifice anyone can offer. He is a poor man, and he hopes he has enough money.
- ☒ First he has to go to a table and change some money. He

is not allowed to use the usual Roman money, only the special Temple money.

☒ Now he has bought the pigeons from a merchant at another table. They were very expensive.

☒ The man and his family go through a gate into a courtyard in front of the Temple. I cannot follow them because I am not a Jew. The mother will stay in the Jewish women's courtyard. Only the man can go through to the inner courtyard and give his sacrifice to the priest.

☒ End of report. Returning to my own time.

FRIENDS 1

JESUS CHOOSES HIS FOLLOWERS

GETTING READY TO HELP WITH ASSEMBLY

We are going to think about friends in our next class assembly. Jesus chose a group of twelve disciples who later became his friends. A disciple means a pupil or student, someone ready to learn.

Job 1

Find the names of Jesus' disciples. Look in the Bible at Luke chapter 6 verses 14–16 for all the names. Fill them in on this chart. Then write the names of Jesus' disciples on large pieces of paper or card to show to the class.

Job 2

Think of the names of twelve people you could work well with and learn alongside. They don't have to be people in your class. Brothers and sisters may be good to learn with, too. Write the names on the chart. In the space under each name, write why you have chosen that person. Are they a good friend? Do they work quietly? Do they share their things? Another reason?

Jesus' disciples	People we would like to work with
S _ _ _ called P _ _ _ _	
A _ _ _ _ _	
J _ _ _	
J _ _	
P _ _ _ _	
B _ _ _ _ _ _	
M _ _ _ _ _	
T _ _ _ _	
J _ _ _ son of A _ _ _ _ _ _	
S _ _ _ the Z _ _ _ _	
J _ _ _ son of J _ _ _ _	
J _ _ _ I _ _ _ _ _	

230

FRIENDS 2

THE FRIENDS WHO ARGUED

GETTING READY TO HELP WITH ASSEMBLY

Do you ever argue with your friends? Jesus' disciples did. You are going to prepare a puppet play about an argument for the next class assembly.

Job 1

Colour and cut out five disciples for the play. Stick a ruler or old paintbrush on the back of each puppet. To stiffen it, mount it on card.

Job 2

Decide how to do the play. It could be two people reading, doing different voices, and two or three others moving the puppets. Or each person could have one puppet and a script to read. Then practise the play, moving the puppets along the road, which is a curtain held up by two people.

Play: The unfriendly argument

(*Puppets appear 'walking' along the road (a curtain held up by two of you).*)

JAMES	I was the first disciple. Jesus came up to me and said, 'Follow me'.
JOHN	Yes. James and I had been fishing and we were sorting out the nets.
JUDAS	What are you two talking about?
JAMES	I think us two are the most important disciples. Jesus chose us first.
PETER	No he didn't. Jesus came to me first, before he had even seen you.

JUDAS	But he has given me the most important job. I look after the money, so I'm the most important disciple.
BARTHOLOMEW	But I'm the oldest. I should be given the best place.
JAMES	No, that's for me. Sitting in heaven, on the Lord's right side!
JOHN	And me on the left. Either side of Jesus, our great leader.
PETER	That's not fair. Why should you two be next to Jesus?
JAMES & JOHN	(*Together, loudly*) Because we're the greatest!
BARTHOLOMEW	You two are so noisy! No wonder you're called Sons of Thunder.
JUDAS	Shh! Look, Jesus is watching us.
BARTHOLOMEW	And he's taking a small child and standing him next to himself.
JOHN	What is he doing that for?
PETER	I think I know what he means. I think he's not going to have *any* of us sit near him if we argue like this.
JAMES & JOHN	Oh dear, we've blown it again! (*Quiet. Puppets walk off.*)

FRIENDS 2

THE FRIENDS WHO ARGUED

Disciple puppets

FRIENDS 3

THE FRIEND WHO BETRAYED JESUS

GETTING READY TO HELP WITH ASSEMBLY

You are going to prepare a short play. It is the night Jesus was arrested. Imagine they had policemen in those days. Police Sergeant Solomon and Constable Amos report to the High Priest about a person they suspect is a criminal.

Job 1

Make a photofit picture of the suspect. He has short black hair, dark skin, and a short beard. He has a large nose, small brown eyes, and a wrinkled forehead. He is dressed in a long middle-eastern robe with a belt. Attached to his belt is a fat purse.

Job 2

Choose three people to be THE CHIEF PRIEST, SERGEANT SOLOMON and CONSTABLE AMOS. Rehearse the play.

Play: The suspect

SERGEANT	Good evening, sir. Sergeant Solomon and Constable Amos of the Jerusalem Police reporting as ordered.
PRIEST	Thank you, Sergeant. We shall need the services of yourself and a small force of armed men tonight.
SERGEANT	Very good, sir. Is it about this sinister character my men have seen hanging around the Temple? We've been keeping a special watch, what with it being the Passover festival, and there being lots of visitors in town. Tell the High Priest what you saw, Constable.
CONSTABLE	Yes, sir. I observed this man behaving suspiciously in the area of the Temple this evening. We've been

keeping an eye on a bunch of trouble-makers this week, and this man is one of them. I'm afraid I lost sight of him for a while. But when I saw him later, he had a large purse on his belt. I'm sure he didn't have that earlier. He could be a thief.

SERGEANT Very good observation, that, Constable Amos. And talking of good observation, show the High Priest the photofit picture we've had drawn of the suspect.

CONSTABLE Yes, sir. Here it is, sir. (*Hold up photofit picture.*) It's a very good likeness.

PRIEST No, no, no! He's not a criminal. He's one of ours. His name is Judas Iscariot. That purse contains thirty pieces of silver I gave him tonight to help us catch the leader of the trouble-makers, Jesus of Nazareth. In fact, I've told him to wait by the Temple courtyard entrance. That's what I want you for, Sergeant. Get a force of armed men. This Judas will lead you to Jesus. I want Jesus arrested and brought here. Quietly. Do you understand?

SERGEANT Yes, sir. Right away, sir.

PRIEST And Sergeant Solomon, don't think for yourself. Just obey orders. Now!

LIFE'S BIG QUESTIONS
ASKING QUESTIONS

GETTING READY TO HELP WITH ASSEMBLY

You are going to help introduce the next class assembly. Your job is to think of some questions to ask the rest of the class. There are three kinds of questions to think of: easy questions, silly questions, and big questions.

Look at the chart. The first column is headed **Easy questions**. There is one easy question already written in that column: 'What colour is grass?' Think of three more easy questions that anyone can answer. Write the questions down.

The next column says **Silly questions**. Silly questions are questions that can't have an answer. There is one silly question written already: 'Where do pineapples lay their eggs?' Another silly question could be: 'What time is a chair-leg?' Think of some more and write them down.

The third column says **Big questions**. Big questions are questions about life and death and God. They are about things that puzzle us and make us think. There is one big question written already: 'Did God make the world or did it just happen?' Another big question could be: 'What happens when someone dies?' Can you think of some more? Write them down.

If you get stuck, you might have to ask your teacher or another grown-up to help.

Choose three people to tell the rest of the class your questions in the next class assembly.

Easy questions	Silly questions	Big questions
1. What colour is grass?	Where do pineapples lay their eggs?	Did God make the world or did it just happen?
2.		
3.		
4.		

LIFE'S BIG QUESTIONS

ASKING QUESTIONS

Blank jigsaw piece

LIFE'S BIG QUESTIONS

WHO MADE GOD?

LIFE'S BIG QUESTIONS

DOES GOD EXIST?

GETTING READY TO HELP WITH ASSEMBLY

You have an exciting job to do to prepare for the next class assembly. You are going to design a house to live in which will care for the environment. We call this **an eco-house.**

An eco-house uses natural resources like the sun, rain, wind and plants. It will be well insulated so as not to waste heat. Kitchen and garden waste will be made into a compost heap and used to grow vegetables. What other ideas can you think of to save energy and prevent waste?

Talk about the ideas you have for your house in your group. Then either draw a large picture of the house and label it, or write some notes about it from your ideas. Get ready to tell the class about your eco-house in the next assembly. One day you might live in a house like this yourself!

LIFE'S BIG QUESTIONS

DOES GOD EXIST?

LIFE'S BIG QUESTIONS

WHAT IS GOD LIKE? 1

LIFE'S BIG QUESTIONS

WHAT IS GOD LIKE? 2

LIFE'S BIG QUESTIONS

WHY AM I HERE?

WHY AM I HERE? 2

Jesus once told his disciples that he was going to heaven to prepare a place for them to be with him. One of the disciples, Simon Peter, later made a list of things to get ready for going to heaven. You are going to help the class next assembly by reading Peter's list. While one of you reads the list, someone else is going to hold up slips of paper with the words on and drop them in a bag.

Job 1

Cut five sheets of paper in half longways to make ten strips. Copy the words in the right-hand column below onto these pieces of paper in big letters using dark colours. There are eight things to write. (The other strips of paper are in case you make a mistake.)

Job 2

Choose a reader to read the words in the left-hand column. Choose a second person to hold up the words on the papers and a third person to hold a bag to put them in.

Job 3

Practise. The reader reads the lines one at a time. The second person holds up the paper with the words on for the class to see, then puts it in the bag.

BEFORE THE READER   faith
STARTS . . .

READER	WORDS
Try as much as you can to add these things to your lives: to your faith, add goodness;	goodness
and to your goodness, add knowledge;	knowledge
and to your knowledge, add self-control;	self-control
and to your self-control, add the ability to hold on;	being able to hold on
and to your ability to hold on, add service for God;	service for God
and to your service for God, add kindness to your brothers and sisters in Christ;	kindness
and to this kindness, add love.	love

LIFE'S BIG QUESTIONS

WHY DO BAD THINGS HAPPEN? 1

LIFE'S BIG QUESTIONS

WHY DO BAD THINGS HAPPEN? 2

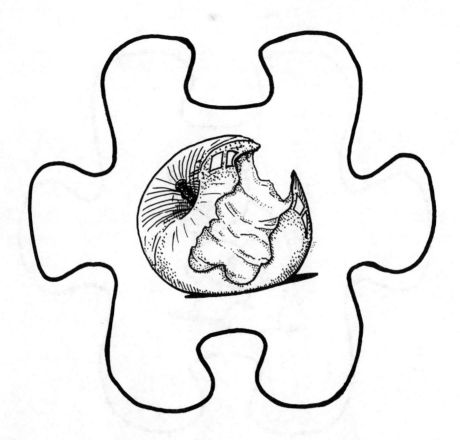

LIFE'S BIG QUESTIONS

WHY DO BAD THINGS HAPPEN? 3

GETTING READY TO HELP WITH ASSEMBLY

You are going to tell the rest of the class about some of the things that happened to Jesus. Decide who is going to read each piece and write the names in the spaces. Practise reading aloud.

Name	**Reading**
. . . .	When Jesus was born, there was no room in the inn. Jesus' family knew what it was like to be homeless.
. . . .	King Herod sent soldiers to kill the babies in Bethlehem. Mary and Joseph had to take Jesus to another country to escape. They knew what it was like to be refugees.
. . . .	Jesus told people lots of things about God and about life, but a lot of important people would not listen. Jesus knew what it was like to tell the truth and not have people believe you.
. . . .	Jesus' cousin, John the Baptist, was killed in prison by another ruler called Herod. Jesus knew what it was like to have a tragic death in the family.
. . . .	Judas betrayed Jesus, and his other friends ran away when the soldiers came to arrest him. Jesus knew what it was like to have friends let you down.

. . . . After Jesus was arrested, people told lies about him and did not give him a fair trial. He knew what it was like to be treated unfairly.

. . . . The soldiers blindfolded Jesus and beat him up and made fun of him. Jesus knew what it was like to be bullied.

. . . . Jesus was hung on a cross and left to die. He knew what it was like to suffer terrible pain.

LIFE'S BIG QUESTIONS

WHY DO BAD THINGS HAPPEN? 3

LIFE'S BIG QUESTIONS

WHY DID MY HAMSTER DIE?

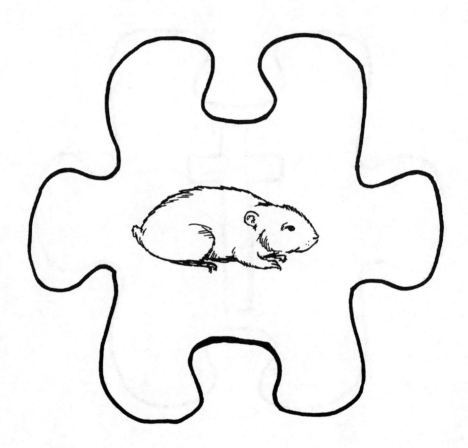